Jesus The Egyptian

Other Books By Richard A. Gabriel

Ancient Empires at War (3 vols) (2005)
Subotai the Valiant: Genghis Khan's Greatest General (2004)
Lion of the Sun (2003)
The Military History of Ancient Israel (2003)
Great Armies of Antiquity (2002)
Sebastian's Cross (2002)
Gods Of Our Fathers (2001)
Warrior Pharaoh (2001)
Great Captains of Antiquity (2000)
Great Battles of Antiquity (1994)
A Short History of War: Evolution of Warfare and Weapons (1994)
History of Military Medicine: Ancient Times to the Middle Ages (1992)
History of Military Medicine: Renaissance to the Present (1992)
From Sumer To Rome: The Military Capabilities of Ancient Armies (1991)
The Culture of War: Invention and Early Development (1990)
The Painful Field: Psychiatric Dimensions of Modern War (1988)
No More Heroes: Madness and Psychiatry in War (1987)
The Last Centurion (French, 1987)
Military Psychiatry: A Comparative Perspective (1986)
Soviet Military Psychiatry (1986)
Military Incompetence: Why The US Military Doesn't Win (1985)
Operation Peace For Galilee: The Israeli-PLO War in Lebanon (1985)
The Antagonists: An Assessment of the Soviet and American Soldier (1984)
The Mind of the Soviet Fighting Man (1984)
Fighting Armies: NATO and the Warsaw Pact (1983)
Fighting Armies: Antagonists of the Middle East (1983)
Fighting Armies: Armies of the Third World (1983)
To Serve With Honor: A Treatise on Military Ethics (1982)
The New Red Legions: An Attitudinal Portrait of the Soviet Soldier (1980)

The New Red Legions: A Survey Data Sourcebook (1980)
Managers and Gladiators: Directions of Change in the Army (1978)
Crisis in Command: Mismanagement in the Army (1978)
Ethnic Groups in America (1978)
Program Evaluation: A Social Science Approach (1978)
The Ethnic Factor in the Urban Polity (1973)
The Environment: Critical Factors in Strategy Development (1973)

Jesus The Egyptian

✦

The Origins of Christianity And The Psychology of Christ

Richard A. Gabriel

iUniverse, Inc.

New York Lincoln Shanghai

Jesus The Egyptian
The Origins of Christianity And The Psychology of Christ

Copyright © 2005 by Richard A. Gabriel

iUniverse books may be ordered through booksellers or by contacting:

iUniverse
2021 Pine Lake Road, Suite 100
Lincoln, NE 68512
www.iuniverse.com
1-800-Authors (1-800-288-4677)

ISBN-13: 978-0-595-35087-2 (pbk)
ISBN-13: 978-0-595-67196-0 (cloth)
ISBN-13: 978-0-595-79789-9 (ebk)
ISBN-10: 0-595-35087-9 (pbk)
ISBN-10: 0-595-67196-9 (cloth)
ISBN-10: 0-595-79789-X (ebk)

Printed in the United States of America

"Homo Sapiens is the species that invents symbols in which to invest passion and authority and then forgets that the symbols are inventions."

Joyce Carol Oates

For Uncle Mickey and Aunt Jane,
My Beloved Godparents,
With Love and Gratitude

Contents

Introduction

It is always difficult to be objective about the life of the founder of a great religion. His personality is blurred by an aura of the miraculous, enhanced inevitably by the needs of the believers to, above all, believe. The earliest biographers, those closest to the time of his life, are preoccupied not with historical facts, but with glorifying in every way the memory of one they believe to have been a Messenger of God or even God himself. The result is a rich accretion of myth and miracle, mysterious portents and heavenly signs, of residues from other religions and religious traditions. These early biographies cannot pass as history; only the propaganda of an expanding faith. It is the task of the historian to locate and explicate the truth that lies behind the myth, to reconstruct the events of a real, as distinct from a symbolic, life. At the root of the effort rests the historian's faith that the task can be accomplished at all.

This book is the result of more than thirty years of study and writing about the world of antiquity, a world that changed markedly with the coming of Jesus Christ. I cannot say with any exactitude just when it was that I began to realize that some of the religious beliefs which heretofore I had associated with my own Catholic faith bore a remarkable similarity to those developed by Egyptian theologians more than two millennia before Jesus appeared on the stage of history. Or when I first became aware of the remarkable intellectual integration with which Egyptian priests thought and wrote about such subjects as creation, the soul, resurrection, judgement beyond the grave, and eternal life. Egyptian thinking on these subjects appeared to me to be theologically indistinguishable from the beliefs that formed the core of my own religious faith, a faith that held that Christianity was a singular historical event without human precedent.

To a person of greater faith this discovery might not have presented a problem. Any similarity between Christianity and Egyptian theology could, after all, be explained away as due to divine contrivance and, thus, without historical meaning. To those of us of lesser conviction, however, the problem remained a nagging one. It bordered on the absurd to assert that the core religious precepts of an ancient Egyptian theological system were identical to those of Christianity if the latter was held to be an historical singularity attributable only to divine causation. It was, I confess, this utter absurdity that provoked me to consider that

1

Christianity as a system of theology might have genuine historical antecedents. It was then that I began the search for the memories of Egypt that seemed to me to rest at the root of the Christian faith.

The purpose of my research was to investigate whether or not there was sufficient evidence for the proposition that the source of Christianity lay heretofore undiscovered within the theologies of ancient Egypt. I will argue here that the principles and precepts of the Osiran theology of Egypt are virtually identical in *content* and *application* to the principles and precepts of Christianity as they present themselves in the Jesus saga. Moreover, the Egyptian theology existed as an unbroken historical thread that began and developed within Egypt for almost three thousand years before being spread across the Mediterranean world by the Greeks until it finally came to rest in the Roman empire and, in particular, in the Palestine of Jesus' day where, if we can trust the saga of the Gospels, it was adopted by Jesus and his followers as a new theological system. One can of course dismiss the argument on the grounds that any similarity of theological principles between pagan Egypt and Christianity is merely accidental and their presence in history millennia before these same principles were revealed directly by God is of no theological relevance whatsoever. The argument, of course, proceeds from faith and involves a form of reasoning that cannot be addressed by the historian. However, the historian is still at liberty to inquire why it might have been that divine revelation was made evident to two different groups of believers at two different times in history?

It was certainly not my purpose in writing this book to challenge religion per se or any particular faith or church. My purpose was to inquire of the available archaeological and historical evidence whether the principal precepts of Christianity could be discovered in Egypt millennia before Christianity claimed them as its own; and whether these core beliefs were conceived and developed by Egyptian theologians before there were any Christian theologians. I am now convinced that this was indeed the case.

Even a very close similarity between cultural artifacts, in this case remarkably similar theological systems, does not make a *prima facie* case that one was derived from the other. The fact that Egyptian civilization was prior in time to the advent of Christianity in Palestine in the first century C.E. certainly makes a stronger case for cross-cultural transfer, but it is by no means entirely convincing by itself. That is why I have attempted to demonstrate that as Christianity arose in Palestine during this time there existed at the same time a *contemporary* theological equivalent in Egypt, an historical reality that renders the idea of the transference of these similar theologies between the two cultures much more likely. Christianity emerged at a time and place when the Osiran theology of Egypt was well-known and commonly practiced both in Palestine and throughout the Roman world. The "new" Christian theology arose within a cultural and historical environment where the Egyptian Osiran theology was powerfully apparent and, perhaps, even dominant in the religious thinking of the day. The influence of Egyptian Osiran theology can therefore be shown to have been contemporaneous with the emergence of Christianity, making it quite likely that any similarities between the two are more than accidental.

The argument rests on two propositions: First, that the pair of theologies, Osiran and Christian, are identical in the *content* and *application* of their respective core theological principles. Second, that Christian theology emerged at a point in history when the influence of its theological predecessor can be shown to have been pervasive upon it and upon the environment in which it emerged, to include Jesus' adoption of a number of ritual practices that were already evident in the Osiran religion while being clearly condemned by the Judaism of his day. Under these circumstances the historian may legitimately assert that both theologies are really cultural artifacts that developed much like other cultural artifacts, and that there is no sound basis upon which to sustain the assumption, probably invented by early adherents of the new Christian theology, that Christianity is revelatory and not historical.

If the argument can be sustained, a further question arises: Given that the Jesus saga presents an account of the origin of Christianity that is at least generally accurate, how are we to explain Jesus' adoption of a pagan Egyptian theology apparently as a reform impulse within Judaism, even as Jesus claimed to be the founder of a "new" religion? Given the historic reality of Jesus, what *human psychological motives* can be discerned from the Gospel saga and other period sources that might explain how a Jew of his times might have rejected his own theological heritage in favor of what was certainly the most widely practiced pagan religion in the Mediterranean world of Jesus' day?

That historians should have overlooked the Egyptian origins of Christianity leaving the subject to the concern of theologians is not terribly surprising. By the middle of the fourth century C.E. Christianity was becoming established in Egypt, but still possessed only a minority following in Egypt and the larger Middle East. The old pagan cults with their ancient systems of temples and priests continued to thrive. Rome was now ruled by Christian emperors, and as Christianity spread throughout the empire pressure increased to deal decisively with the old cults, particularly the Osiran-Isis cult that seems to have been the major competitor for converts. (1) Although it was not yet so, Christianity was becoming the majority religion of the empire and was ready to assert itself by force and violence. The spark was provided by the desert monks of the Christian ascetic movement who urged a campaign of liquidation against their pagan competitors.

In 356 C.E. Constantius II ordered the Egyptian temples of Isis-Osiris closed and forbade the use of Egyptian hieroglyphics as a religious language. In 380 C.E. Emperor Theodosius declared Christianity to be the official Roman state religion, and all pagan cults were thereafter forbidden. These edicts were devastating to Egyptian culture and religion, both of which had been preserved over millennia through the Egyptian language and the writing systems of Egyptian priests. In 391 C.E. the Patriarch of Alexandria, Theophilus, summoned the monks to arms and turned them against the city of Memphis and the great shrine of Serapis, the *Serapeum*, the main temple of the Osiran-Isis religion. The attack was akin to ordering the destruction of the Vatican. Egyptian priests were massacred in their shrines and in the streets. The ferocity of the violence consumed priests, followers, and the Egyptian intellectual elite of Alexandria, Memphis, and the other cities of Egypt who were murdered and their temples and libraries destroyed. The institutional structure of Egyptian religion, then more than four millennia old, was demolished in less than two decades. The wave of religious terrorism that swept Egypt for twenty years seemed to some Egyptians to herald the end of the world. *"If we are alive,"* one wrote, *"then life itself is dead."* (2) At Philae, the last temple to Isis where the liturgy was still pronounced in Egyptian and hieroglyphics were still written was closed in the mid-sixth century. From that time forward, a veil of silence was drawn over Egyptian history leaving only legends in the memory of the West.

All serious intellectual inquiry begins with assumptions about the nature of the subject examined. The disciplines of history and theology are no exceptions. If we begin with the assumption that the origins of Christianity lie within divine revelation, then a range of questions are *ab initio* placed beyond further analysis. If Christianity is seen as the product of God's intervention in the affairs of men, then we might never ask what is to be made of the stark theological similarities between Christianity and Osirism. It is always possible that these and other questions might well prove to be worthless inquiries. But we shall never know this unless we are permitted to pose them.

The analysis offered here is not an assault upon religion, and not a single word is offered regarding the truth or falsity of any religious precept or belief examined here. Neither is the analysis theological, and no conclusion is offered as to the validity of any theological proposition, Egyptian or Christian. The analysis is most properly viewed as a treatment in the *history of theology*, an approach that offers a perspective from which the reader may examine the origins of Christianity as *artifacts of history* rather than as *artifacts of faith*. If the subject were pottery, temple ruins, or ancient documents, it is unlikely that anyone would object to the form of historical analysis offered here. One might imagine, too, that the elements of evidence proffered would be more easily accepted as methods of proof if the subject were any ancient artifact other than religion. It is important to remember that the subject of this book resides in the domain of history, not in the realm of faith.

NOTES

1. Peter Brown, *The World of Late Antiquity* (New York: W.W. Norton, 1989), 100.

2. While the influence of Isis during the time of Jesus will be addressed further in what follows, for support of the proposition that it was the most popular religion in the ancient world during Christ's time, see R.E. Witt, *Isis in the Ancient World* (Baltimore, MD: Johns Hopkins University Press, 1971) in its entirety.

1

Egyptian Gifts

Only when human beings become aware of the inner voice that we call conscience does a social group begin moving toward civilization. It is then that man begins to discover what separates him from the beasts, a difference that makes possible the contemplation of moral qualities like justice, charity, mercy, and forgiveness. From this discovery of our own moral intuition, what Breasted calls the "dawn of conscience," (1) arises our ability to fashion gods in our own image, to make idealized versions of ourselves, so that by emulating them we become more like our better selves. Without the dawn of conscience, the history of humanity would have been but a long dark night.

Where do we find the first evidence of humans struggling to discover and develop their moral sense? The answer is not in the West, although that is the common view. It is often assumed that the age of moral reasoning found its first flicker in the Age of Revelation with the emergence of the *Decalogue of Moses* and the ethical postulates that attended the founding of Judaism. This stream of moral awareness, so the argument goes, was expanded by the revelations of Christianity and the Gospels forming the core of Western moral thinking. This argument offers a myopic Western view of itself as the center of all things great, and is simply false. The West is surely *not* where mankind's moral conscience first emerged. It was in Egypt, long before there was a West at all, three thousand years before there were any Israelites, and four thousand years before there were any Christians, that evidence for the first stirring of moral conscience is found.

There are only two civilizations sufficiently old to qualify as the source of ethical thinking: Egypt and Mesopotamia. Both emerged about six thousand years ago and developed writing and man's first serious theologies at about the same time. But it was Egypt that gave the world the gift of conscience. The circumstances of Egyptian development laid the basis for a society in which moral awareness, intellectual inquiry, and theological speculation flourished. By the end of the Stone Age desiccation around the Nile Valley turned the grasslands to

desert forcing men and animals closer to the river. By the sixth millennium
B.C.E. agriculture and animal husbandry were common. The soil was rich and
the Nile's watery abundance constantly threatened to overrun the land. By 5000
B.C.E. Egypt possessed a million souls living in villages and towns along the Nile.
One of the predynastic kings, probably Scorpion, set out to construct a massive
irrigation system to control the Nile flood. The Nile runs for more than seven
hundred miles, and to control its waters required the cooperation or conquest of
the entire area.

Egypt was divided into a number of feudal baronies (*nomes*) each possessing its
own capital, army, local god, and powerful chieftain. Scorpion unified the *nomes*
by force and established Egypt's first national government. Around this time the
local sun god of Heliopolis, Re, was transformed into a national god. Some powerful prince of Heliopolis whose name remains unknown brought the sun god
into the realm of secular affairs imposing on the unified country the idea that the
king was the son of god. The installation of Re, *"he who overlooks all gods; there is
no god who overlooks thee,"* as a national deity who intervened in the secular affairs
of men was of great importance. The desire of Re that men do *Maat* (right, justice, fairness) became the most basic ethical precept of the Egyptian state. Re's
command that humans do what is right on this earth is the earliest Egyptian ethical precept known to us. The precept is, of course, still linked to a divine command. Humans are not yet ready to consider their own experience as the source
of judgement. But some six thousand years ago in Egypt they have taken the first
step. (2)

The First Union lasted for several centuries before conflict among the feudal
nomes forged two great coalitions into two independent kingdoms. The center of
the northern kingdom was the town of Dep in the Nile Delta where the cobra
goddess was worshipped. This was the kingdom of the Red Land. The southern
kingdom had its capital at Nekhen (near Hieraconopolis) and was called the
White Land. Here the vulture god, Nekhbet, was worshipped. (3) Sometime
around 3400 B.C.E. a powerful king named Narmer rose to power in the southern kingdom and conquered the kingdom of the north becoming the founder of
the First Dynasty. As a symbol of unification, the great king moved his capital
from Nekhbet to a new location at the neck of the Delta where the southern
lands begin, and constructed the City of the White Walls, Memphis, that
remained the capital of Egypt for the next seventeen hundred years. Thus arose
the first great civilized state at a time when most of Asia and Europe were still
inhabited by scattered communities of Stone Age hunters.

The unification of Egypt brought into being a large, rich, peaceful kingdom with a national government and national culture. Where Mesopotamia's kings had brought civil war, Egypt's leaders brought civil peace. Unlike Mesopotamia which was further disturbed for more than a thousand years by periodic invasions and civil wars, Egypt was blessed by geography with secure and nearly impenetrable borders. Great deserts to the west and east were formidable barriers to invasion. To the south the Nile's passage through Aswan and Elephantine afforded protection by swift rapids and easily defended natural strongpoints. To the north the Mediterranean Sea, what Egyptians called the Great Green, also protected Egypt. The result was a nation that was almost hermetically sealed, self-sufficient in food, well-governed, prosperous, and secure. A thousand years of peace provided the environment for contemplating morality and religion. No culture on earth was more sophisticated in its religious and moral thinking than Egypt.

It is likely that the human contemplation of religion was the first stimulus that led to an awareness of the inner moral voice that lies at the root of conscience from which moral and ethical thinking eventually arose. Egyptian attempts to discern the mind of god led inevitably to a reflective morality that stimulated humans to think about right conduct for the first time in history. The point of moral reference was still the mind of god; but the process of ethical evolution had begun. Humans produced the first moral treatise in Egypt at the beginning of the Old Kingdom or Pyramid Age (2780-2250 B.C.E.) in a document called the *Memphite Drama*. It constitutes the earliest known discussion of right and wrong in the history of humankind. (4)

The treatise describes events that can only be found in the period of the Second Union or about 3400 B.C.E., (5) and is presented in dramatic form like the Christian mystery plays of the Middle Ages which employed drama to frame the discussion of important moral lessons. The *Drama* is a semi-theological, semi-philosophical discussion of the origins and moral responsibilities of man, and is the first written evidence of man's propensity for moral discernment. The *Drama* was produced by a priestly body of temple thinkers at Memphis and begins with an explanation of the creation of the universe by Ptah, a local god that the priests had raised to the status of a national deity to replace the old sun god Re, whose powers were not diminished but merely assumed by Ptah. The *Memphite Drama* is the first attempt in human history to conceive of a civic moral order as an integral part of a cosmic moral order, and for a thousand years the ideas expressed in this seminal document shaped the manner of Egyptian political and moral life until the end of the Pyramid Age (2250 B.C.E.) brought forth further refinement of its ethical concepts.

The *Drama* is evidence of complex abstract thinking about the most difficult subjects. Egyptian thinkers see a world that is operating intelligibly and are trying to discern how and why the order they see about them exists. It is, they decide, the product of the will of Ptah from which everything comes and by which everything is kept alive. The world is brought into being by an active intelligence who keeps it going. Ptah is the creator and animator of all life, human and otherwise. The act of creation is remarkably conceived by the Egyptian thinkers who reckon that Ptah made everything that exists *by the agency of his mind*, that is, first he thought of the thing to be created and then willed it to come into being. By calling out the names of things Ptah caused them to exist, for all things *"came into being through that which the heart (the mind to the Egyptians) thought and the tongue (speech) commanded."* (6) The obvious similarity of this idea to the Christian concept of creation is striking, for here we see what appears to be the *Logos* doctrine of creation expressed in the Gospel of St. John.

John describes the act of creation in the following way: *"In the beginning was the Word, and the Word was with God, and the Word was God. The same was in the beginning with God. All things were made by him; and without him was not any thing made that was made. In Him was life; and the life was the life of men."* (7) Some scholars, like the renowned E.A. Wallis Budge, find in the *Memphite Drama* the first expression of Egyptian monotheism. According to Budge, "the priests of Ptah had at that time arrived at the highest conception of God which was ever reached in Egypt, and their religion was a pure monotheism. They evolved the idea of God as Spirit, a self-created, self-subsisting, eternal almighty mind-god, the creator of all things, the source of all life and creation, who created everything that is merely by thinking…the Word which gave expression to the thought which "came into his mind." (8) The Egyptians were affirming the existence of a cosmic moral order, an order governed by laws of right conduct where God approves of some actions and disapproves of others, where *"life is given to the peaceful and death is given to the guilty."* The good man does *"that which is loved"* and the evil man *"does what is hated."*

The tendency toward monotheism in Egyptian religion is very old. Paradoxically, it was the tolerance of Egyptian *polytheism* for many gods that led eventually to Egyptian *monotheistic* thinking to discern the nature of god. The Egyptians understood that the local gods were very different from the major gods in the same way, perhaps, that Christian saints differ from the deity itself. The Egyptians arrived at the proposition early on that all gods were but different manifestations or permitted forms of the same one god. The observance of the "many" gave rise to the belief in the "One" god, and to the Egyptian idea that

"The All is One," which finds its Greek resonance in the idea of the cosmological unity of being. (9) According to Egyptian thinking, the one god possessed the following characteristics. He is a god: (1) whose birth is secret; (2) whose place of origin is unknown; (3) whose birth is not witnessed; (4) who created himself by himself; and (5) who keeps his nature concealed from all who come after him. (10) He is "the Hidden One" who exists and is the source of all else. It was the events of the later Imperial Age (1552-1188 B.C.E.) that brought into existence a national priesthood that emphasized the *universality* of god in a more powerful expression of the monotheistic tendency that had always marked Egyptian thinking since the days of the Ptah ascendancy more than a thousand years earlier.

The new emphasis on monotheistic elements in Egyptian religion led to a renewed emphasis on another ancient idea, the trinity. Egyptian theologians conceived the idea of a trinitarian god as an answer to one of the basic questions that had concerned them for hundreds of years. How could the many gods of the Egyptian pantheon be reconciled with the idea of one god? It was clear to them that a single deity stood behind all creation. The original stimulus for the concept was the Egyptian practice of elevating the status of a local god by associating it with a powerful and recognized national god. At first the Egyptians simply joined the gods in modalistic trinities in which the supreme deity manifested itself in different "modes" of the lesser gods. (11) Thus, the sun was seen as a trinity manifesting itself in three modes, morning, afternoon, and evening. These first attempts were abandoned even before the Pyramid Age ended, as the *Memphite Drama* demonstrates. What they reveal, however, is that very early on Egyptian theologians were thinking about a unity that must lie behind the plurality of all existence. Egyptian theologians went on to evolve a theology of the basic unity of a single god. They conceived of the one god as trinity to reconcile this intrinsic unity with the complexity of existence that they saw all around them. (12)

The Egyptian idea of a trinitarian god is perhaps the most sophisticated theological concept found in any society of the ancient world, and Egyptian explanations of its nature are as sophisticated as any philosophical discourse to emerge in any later period of intellectual history, including the complex theology accompanying the Christian idea of its own trinitarian god. The Egyptians conceived of a union of important national gods that were different manifestations or persons within a single deity. This union was not static, but a "dynamic inhabitation" that did not limit the independence, action, or nature of the joined persons. (13) All persons within the trinity remained identifiable and possessed of their own natures and were all equally divine. This "indwelling" was an idea that Egyptian theologians applied to the images of their gods as well, and represents the earliest known thinking about incarnation, where god becomes manifest in something material. Statues of the gods were believed to be fully alive incarnations of the deity itself.

The Egyptian notion of incarnation is likely to strike the modern reader as absurd. But one need only enter a Catholic church to see that the idea of indwelling (*incarnatio*) is very much with us. Every Catholic church possesses a monstrance, a golden disc about a foot in diameter with suns rays emanating from its center that sits on a golden stand. At the center of the monstrance is a transparent glass circle in which the communion host of unleavened bread resides. This is the Holy Eucharist. Catholic theology holds that this blessed bread is the body of Jesus himself. That is, the bread host is *not a symbol of Jesus' body but the body itself* that "dwells" in the bread host in precisely the same manner that the Egyptians believed the body of their god to be "dwelling" in the sacred statue of the god. The monstrance is brought out with great reverence and ceremony upon special days of the year and presented to the congregation in a manner strongly reminiscent of the Egyptian priests presenting the image of their god to their congregations during worship. Since each church has a monstrance, like the ancient gods of Egypt, the body of Jesus is believed to "dwell" in more than one place at the same time just as an Egyptian god "dwelled" in its image at different temples at one and the same time.

The unique nature of the Egyptian trinitarian god is that the trinity was conceived of as a singularity, as a unity that encompassed within it the plurality of the other gods while remaining distinct itself. This singularity was reflected linguistically in the Egyptian use of the singular pronoun "He" when applied to god as trinity (14) in much the same manner as the Christian God is referred to as "He" when "He" is seen to be comprised of three distinct persons, the Father, Son, and Holy Spirit. The "He" of the Christians and the "He" of the Egyptians are both singularities representing solutions to the search for unity that was thought to underlie the complexity of all existence.

The trinitarian conception of god is first found during the early Pyramid Age when the *Memphite Drama* described the union of Ptah with Sokaris and Osiris. There were other Egyptian trinities throughout the centuries, but none was seen as the equal of Ptah. With the ascendancy of Re in the Feudal Age (2200-2040 B.C.E.), the trinitarian idea receded into the background as Re himself became perceived as the supreme god. The renewed emphasis on a trinitarian god during the Imperial Age was a consequence of the desire of the Theban princes to elevate the Theban city god, Amun, to the status of the older and greater Re, with the result that a new trinity was born. Re and Amun were joined with Ptah, the oldest and most prominent god. The Christian idea of "three persons in one god" and the Egyptian idea of "All is One" were clearly reflected in the New Kingdom hymn to the new trinity: *"All gods are three: Amun, Re, and Ptah; and there is no second to them. Hidden is His name as Amun, He is Re in fact, and His body is Ptah."* (15) The idea of god as trinity has no counterpart in any other religious belief system in the ancient world. It appears nowhere else in history until Christian times when the idea comes to form a central mystery of Christian theology.

The *Memphite Drama* is the earliest discussion of right conduct and constitutes the earliest example of man's ability to draw the distinction between that which is good and that which is not. It is truly the event horizon of man's moral thinking, the first attempt to think in abstract ethical terms and to judge his own behavior precisely in those terms. It is a marvelous moment and it is happening for the first time in human history as far as we know. The *Drama* also contains within it the seeds of a larger *societal* ethic that eventually emerged at a later date. From the dawn of time the Egyptians believed their king to be divine, while remaining no less a creation of god than other creatures. If god commands that men do certain things and not others, then surely this applies to the sovereign as well. The sovereign was therefore charged with being a righteous ruler in a politico-social sense and bore the responsibility to see that *Maat* (justice, right, righteousness) was done because god desired it. Here for the first time is the core of the doctrine that the power of the sovereign may be limited by ethical precept, an idea that later occupied Western political thinkers for centuries.

It was only a few centuries after the *Memphite Drama* that other ethical texts began to make their appearance. Among the most important of these were the *Maxims of Ptahhotep* (Circa B.C.E. or even older) (16) which provides us with the specifics of what right conduct meant to the Egyptians of the period. The *Maxims* take the form of a letter written by an ageing government official to his son who he hopes will succeed him in his post and offers advice on how to behave properly. It is a prescription for right conduct, the oldest formulation of right conduct found in any literature. (17) The *Maxims of Ptahotep* is the earliest surviving example of what are called the "wisdom texts," a body of Egyptian literature comprised of letters, plays, moral tales, and stories stressing right conduct.

The wisdom texts are only one source of our knowledge of how the Egyptians saw their world. The Pyramid Texts are another. During the Pyramid Age powerful Egyptian kings constructed massive pyramid tombs and funerary temples to protect their mummified bodies so that their souls might achieve everlasting life. The idea of an afterlife was present very early in Egypt and was well-established even in pre-dynastic times, as was the practice of providing the deceased with sustenance to support him in the afterlife. (18) From pre-dynastic times to the end of the Pyramid Age an afterlife spent in the presence of the gods was thought to be reserved for the king and his powerful barons, and had not yet been extended to include all men. The theological system of the Memphite priests taught that *all* men must do *Maat*, and the idea developed early that the sovereign would be subject to judgement after death by the god who would assess the moral quality of his life on earth. Egyptian kings had records of their lives and good deeds inscribed on the walls of their tombs so that the gods might know of the proper moral quality of their lives and render a favorable judgement. These funerary inscriptions were idealized biographies of the deceased testifying to good conduct and are highly ethical in tone and content. Carved in stone, thousands of these tomb inscriptions, called the Pyramid Texts, provide us with a valuable insight into Egyptian moral thinking.

It is in these inscriptions that we find the earliest utterances of humans that they could be called to answer for their actions and that their actions on this earth might determine their eternal fate. This is a vitally important idea and completely original as far as we know. It holds humans responsible for their conduct, and it is this responsibility and free will that rest at the center of all human ethics. Nowhere else do we find such thinking at so early a date. In Mesopotamia man conceived of no such judgement. After death both vicious and virtuous alike were consigned to a Hades-like existence regardless of the moral quality of their lives. Two thousand years after the Egyptians the Israelites came to recognize the value of an ethical life but did not connect it with either an afterlife or a moral judgement of the deceased. It was not until the advent of Christianity, three thousand years after the first Egyptian ethical thinkers, that the world again witnessed an ethical doctrine that determined one's place in eternity on the basis of moral behavior in this life.

Not surprisingly Egyptian moral behavior was originally rooted within the family which stood at the center of Egyptian life. The idea of right conduct gradually spread to the treatment of other men (social ethics) and eventually, under the stimulus of the judgement of the god, to the king and the powerful (political ethics). These developments were accompanied by similar developments in the wisdom literature until the expectation of moral behavior on the part of the powerful became widespread among the populace. The proposition that the king had moral responsibilities to his subjects, and that the exercise of power was accordingly limited by them, represents the dawn of a radically new idea found nowhere else in the ancient world at this time. For the first time in human history we find the doctrine that political legitimacy depends upon the moral behavior of the ruler and on the moral content of his laws and judgements. Here, two thousand years before Plato, is the core idea of *The Republic*.

The Egyptian concept of law was strongly influenced by Egyptian ethics. Early on Egyptians rejected the idea, common in history for the next four millennia, that law was merely the expressed will of the powerful sovereign. The responsibility of the Egyptian king to do justice extended to making certain that the evil done by other men did not go unpunished. The exercise of justice (*Maat*) required that the law be just in both content and exercise, otherwise the king himself would be morally culpable in failing to do his ethical duty. In Egypt, everyone was subject to the same law in the same way regardless of social standing or wealth. This included women, children, and foreigners. Egypt developed a sophisticated multi-level system of courts and magistrates to hear cases, and the availability of the system to the common man is demonstrated by the thousands of court documents that have survived recording the arguments of the litigants and the decisions rendered. (19) That justice rather than power was at the center of Egyptian law was demonstrated symbolically by the fact that the king's vizier and chief legal officer had the official title of "priest of *Maat*," and court judges wore an image of *Maat* on a gold chain around their necks as a sign of their office. (20) It was Egypt that gave the world the vision of a society governed by just laws and limited sovereign power.

Having derived many of our ethical ideas from the Greeks, the Egyptian idea of ethics was broader than what we in the West are accustomed to. In both cases ethics involves a concern for right conduct. But Egyptian ethics also includes matters that Westerners would normally ascribe to religion. For ancient Egyptians the question of how to treat a person in business, how to do what the gods wish a person to do, and how to address the gods properly in prayer were all equally ethical concerns. At the center of each set of concerns is the moral concept of *Maat*, the earliest abstract term found in any language of antiquity.

What did *Maat* mean to the Egyptian mind? The term itself originally derives from a concrete geometrical or physical term meaning "straightness" or "evenness" in the way that a straight edge or a ruler is useful in determining whether a thing is straight or true. But in the ethical sense *Maat* means much more than to do what is right. *Maat* means also the just order established by god in nature and society through the act of creation. It is the dynamic order that is behind *all* creation, an order humans must strive to preserve by conducting themselves properly toward God, their fellow humans, and all things, even animals. For the Egyptian all life was of a single piece governed by the same moral law. This idea is very close to the Medieval notion of a natural moral order that is the material

expression of the divine order in which human law and human action are partici-
pants in and reflections of the larger order of the universe.

Unlike the later Aristotelian concept, in the Egyptian view the cosmic order
does not govern itself, nor is it governed by some Unmoved Mover. When men
do evil they bring disorder to the natural order of things. Accordingly, it is *man's*
responsibility to preserve and restore the natural order by doing what is right.
Without human moral action, disorder would threaten everything. When men
act properly they are doing precisely what god wants them to do. But Egyptian
ethical thinkers did not conceive of man as merely a servant of the gods as the
Babylonians did. For Egyptians, men were free to choose their fate. To do *Maat*
made humans good in themselves, for living an ethical life was the best way to
live.

To conceive of *Maat* as a basic value achievable by human action has significant consequences for how the Egyptians understood the role of law. The laws of
Egypt were not conceived of as divine injunctions as, for example, the *Decalogue
of Moses* in the Old Testament does. Instead, laws are edicts fashioned by the king
"in the exercise of his supreme power, but by virtue of his insight into the nature
of *Maat*." (21) Law is man-made not god-sent, and its purpose is to guide
humans to reduce disorder in the world by doing what is right. To be sure law is
participatory in the grand ideal of *Maat* by which standard human law may be
judged as good or bad. But it is human law fashioned by human minds nonetheless that brings about justice in the world. Justice is a product of human activity,
and it is humans and not god who bear the ultimate moral responsibility for the
justice or injustice of law.

Egyptian ethics was really an ethic of the mind, a disposition to think about
what is right and a propensity to act upon it because to do so was part of the natural order of the cosmos. The requirement that the general moral maxim be
applied in specific circumstances through the use of reason and free will meant
that the consequences of one's actions must be taken into account. An integral
part of the human moral calculus was the effect one's action had upon other
members of society. There could be no question of ignoring the effects of one's
actions on the ground that one was following divine will or, more pragmatically,
that one had good intentions. Though Egyptian ethics focused upon human
actions, both of omission and commission, they also had a healthy regard for the
facts and mental attitudes that influenced human behavior. Thus a joining
together of *intentions* and *consequences* in assessing the good or evil of human
actions must be counted as a remarkable advance made first by the Egyptians in
the continuing moral discourse that has accompanied human history ever since.

Comprehending ethics in this way led the Egyptians to a unique view of sin. Unlike the Israelites and early Christians, the Egyptians did not believe that sin represented a transgression of divine law nor was sin a personal ritual affront to the gods as the Babylonians believed. There was no expectation that the gods would punish sin on this earth. There are no instances in Egyptian theology that parallel the murderous punishments of Yahweh against the sinners among his own people. (22) Egyptians condemned sin for more pragmatic reasons, that it injured other people and even oneself by destroying one's reputation and character. There was no idea in Egyptian thinking of sin as ontological stain. (23) No one but the individual himself caused sin and no one but the individual was responsible for it. The idea of a sinful human nature central to Christian ethics but unconvincing to Judaism was completely absent from Egyptian moral thinking.

For Egyptians the range of human conduct governed by ethical principles was very broad and included man's conduct toward his fellows, the gods, society, and even animals and natural things like precious water and trees that bore fruit. (24) At the same time a religious impetus for ethical conduct is evident. The Egyptian felt strongly that by doing *Maat* he was doing what god wanted him to do, and he prayed to his god for guidance in doing what was right. In this sense Christian and Egyptian ethics share an important similarity. In both, ethics is more than an intellectual perception and exercise attained by insight and experience. In both there is a strong charismatic and transcendent element in that in trying to do what is right one might reasonably call upon god to help one determine what to do and find the strength to do it. For both there is a striving to do right on earth that is connected with a striving for salvation (doing what god wants) through knowledge and action. For Egyptians and Christians ethics comes to involve intellectual, charismatic, and even magical elements that affect the way humans think and act. (25)

The religious dimension of ethical awareness was never very far from the surface of Egyptian life. The most influential of these dimensions was the belief in an afterlife contingent upon a final judgement of human conduct after death. In assessing the importance of the afterlife in Egyptian thinking the famous Egyptologist James H. Breasted noted that "among no people, ancient or modern, has the idea of a life beyond the grave held so prominent a place as among the ancient Egyptians." (26) We do not know the origins of the Egyptian belief in an afterlife. Perhaps it arose as a consequence of man's recognition of his own mortality, and that awareness led him to want to live forever. Perhaps thinking about it convinced him that it was possible to do so. Whatever its origin, the evidence is clear that the Egyptians were the first humans to systematically think and write about immortality.

The idea of an afterlife was originally confined to the Egyptian king who was seen as the son of god. It was expected that upon his death Pharaoh would return to his place among the gods from which he had come. The notion that the son of god returned to his heavenly father is also found in other cultures where it manifested itself as human sacrifice, most often of the first son (the "first fruits" of the Old Testament) who was thought to be a gift of the god and, thus, needed to be returned to his rightful divine father. (27) While human sacrifice was practiced all over the ancient Near East, the near-sacrifice of Isaac by Abraham being the most famous incident, it never took hold in Egypt. Only the Egyptian king could achieve immortality, and very early on the idea was closely connected with the belief that the body must be preserved for this immortality to be continue. The great expression of this belief in external material means of sustaining immortality is found in the construction of the pyramid tombs. These "Houses of a Million Years" along with specific funerary rituals sought to preserve the king's body and see to his spiritual and material needs in the next world. Originally reserved for the king, the prospect of an afterlife was gradually extended to others until it became the hope of every common Egyptian.

The Pyramid Texts provide us with the oldest surviving portrayals of man's conception of an afterlife. It was a celestial afterlife, one that existed in the sky or "up above," not surprisingly for a people who worshiped the sun, and an idea that reappears much later in Christian thinking. The dead god-king returns to his proper place, to live with the gods in paradise, where he undergoes ritual purification with water in the sacred lake and then "mingles" with the very body and being of Re himself. The idea of "mingling" with god is a very mysterious concept and may represent an idea left over from the time when Egyptians practiced cannibalism! (28) A very old Egyptian hymn may be recalling precisely these ancient practices when it tells of a time when the Great God hunted down the lesser gods, killed them, cooked and ate them to incorporate their goodness and other qualities into his own being. (29) However it was to be achieved, there is a sense in which the king "becomes one with god" and lives forever. The core of this idea can still be found in modern times whenever Christians speak of their anticipated union with god after death.

The intellectual sophistication of Egyptian priests is adequately demonstrated by the fact that by the 30th century B.C.E. they had worked out the main outline of how the afterlife was to be achieved and developed a psychology of the dead to support it. To the Egyptian it was obvious that a person possessed both a visible body and an invisible intelligence, the heart. The combined entity, body and heart, comprised the *Ba*, symbolized by a small human-headed bird always portrayed as hovering over the corpse at death. (30) The *Ba* came into existence only after the person died, but did not become a soul until the body was preserved and restored to animation by funerary prayer and ritual. Thus it was that the priest pronounced these words over the deceased: *"Raise thee up, for this is thy bread, which cannot dry up, and thy beer which cannot become stale, by which thou shalt become a soul."*(31) Once these rites were performed, the body was said to live on and not decay.

The *Ba*'s continued existence depended upon the physical maintenance of the body in the tomb. If the body was destroyed, the *Ba* ceased to exist. In this sense early Egyptian ideas of the soul did not yet regard it as a truly immortal entity, but something still dependent upon the body for its existence. It is apparent that immortality depends upon the maintenance of the externals of life, that is, the security of the tomb, the physical integrity of the body, and even its physical sustenance by daily offerings of bread and beer for eternity. The Egyptians eventually realized that these external mechanisms would be impossible to sustain forever. Once this became evident, as it did at the end of the Pyramid Age, the search began for other means to sustain the soul after death, and the belief in externals was slowly abandoned. Man was about to shift his moral gaze inward, to a time when his inner voice would come to determine and direct all that lay beyond the externals of his life.

The idea of an afterlife brought with it the problem of determining who would be saved and who would not. Although Egyptian kings were the sons of god, they were no less his creations than other creatures and just as required to do *Maat*. If the heavenly life was a continuation of this one as Egyptians believed, then the injunction to do *Maat* must hold in the hereafter as well. As there are human courts so there must be a heavenly court. Amazingly this implies that ethical norms, i.e., those by which a person's soul is judged, take precedence over judicial ones, for the latter deal only with material matters. Early on the Egyptians had developed the idea that there might well be some judgement of the powerful after death to call to account those who had not conducted themselves properly in this life. It required more than a thousand years for Egyptian thinkers to work out the details of this judgement.

It was during the Pyramid Age that the judgement of the dead came to center upon Osiris, the god of the dead. Rosalie David suggests that Osiris was originally a god of vegetation; the Egyptians deduced his nature from the agricultural cycle where plants grow, reproduce, and die only to grow again next season as the periodic Nile flood renews them each year. (32) The Osiris myth took on the form of a religious doctrine that affirmed resurrection and life everlasting. The earliest reference to Osiris is found in the *Memphite Drama* where he is portrayed as sprouts of wild wheat to explain how Memphis became the granary of Egypt. (33) The details of how Osiris became the judge of the dead will be dealt with more fully later. It is sufficient here to note that the theology of an afterlife and judgement connected to Osiris was expressed in the early Pyramid Age when Ptah was combined with Sekar, the god of the dead of Memphis, and Osiris in one of the earliest expressions of the Egyptian idea of god as trinity. (34)

The incorporation of Osiris into the trinitarian god of Ptah represents the growing importance of a belief that reached beyond the Ptah mythology and, eventually, beyond the religion of Re as well. The promise of resurrection and judgement central to the Osiris myth struck deep roots among the populace and eventually became the dominant faith of the common man. Even the solar mythology of Re became "Osirized" in that Osiris was absorbed into the Re theology. When the king arose from the dead he was said to "mingle" with Osiris and actually become him. The growing importance of Osiris in the Re theology is evident in the tomb inscriptions of this time. A curious duality in Egyptian religion emerges. The solar faith of Re remains the official religion of the state and of the foremost theological colleges and seminaries even as the belief in the Osiris faith continues to spread among the general populace. The appeal of resurrection and fair judgement to the common man will eventually win out, so that by the Middle Kingdom (2040 B.C.E.) Osiris is completely merged into the official state worship of Re. By this time belief in resurrection and judgment *for all men* had found official expression in the formal religion of the Egyptian state. In this revised theology Re remains supreme, perhaps in the same sense that in Christian thinking *God the Father* is somehow prior to the *Holy Spirit*, while at the same time both remain equals in their divinity and power.

In Egyptian thinking emerging at the beginning of the Feudal Age (2200 B.C.E.) Re remains the great creator and ruler of the universe just as Ptah had been in the old Memphite cosmology now taken over by the priests of Re at Heliopolis. It is still Re's moral imperative, the command to do *Maat,* that governs the lives of humans on this earth. Re guides the affairs of living men; Osiris guides the affairs of the dead.

The development of Egyptian ethical thought proceeded apace for more than a thousand years before the idea that a judgement after death might influence the eternal fate of the common man found official expression in Egyptian theology. This suggests that while the notion of a judgement after death certainly came to influence ethical thinking on proper conduct in this world, the fundamentals of Egyptian ethical belief and reasoning were formed well before this. The Egyptians had come to the conclusion that a moral life was worth living both for itself and for its beneficial effects on society without any insight provided by Osiran mythology. Morenz in his treatment of Egyptian religion supports the idea that ethical thinking came before the idea of a judgement and that, in his view, the element of a judgement made sense in the Egyptian moral calculus precisely because good men were sometimes treated unjustly in this life. (35) Osiris expanded Egyptian ethical thinking by resolving the problem of injustice on earth by providing for a just final judgement in the hereafter. As the Pyramid Age drew to a close the Re theology recognized that the old idea of immortality achieved through material mechanical means was insufficient and set upon new ways to determine how men might properly behave on this earth so as to merit immortality beyond the grave.

The period from 2200-2040 B.C.E. in Egyptian history is known as the First Intermediate Period or Feudal Age, a time of great trouble for Egypt. The Old Kingdom ended with the death of Pepy II who had a long and ineffectual reign. (36) The Second Union which had lasted for more than a thousand years and had witnessed man's first attempts at moral contemplation collapsed in violence. The monarchy gave way to the growing rivalry and power of the feudal barons of the *nomes* plunging Egyptian society into intermittent civil war. The vital national irrigation system was disrupted causing economic depression and periodic famine. Law and order collapsed and bandits roamed the countryside and towns. Egypt's weakness tempted her bedouin enemies, and there is evidence that parts of the Delta were invaded by Asiatics during this time. (37) The southern half of the country fell away and established itself as a separate kingdom, while a series of strong kings at Herakleopolis finally reestablished order in the north. Conflict between the two realms exploded into open civil war when the Theban kings attempted to unify the country by force. The troubled times of the Feudal Age provoked a new wave of wisdom literature that continued the development of Egyptian moral thinking as it tried to come to grips with the difficult circumstances of the day.

Among the earliest of the Feudal Age wisdom texts is the *Instruction of Merikere* whose author may well have been one of the last Herakleopolitan kings giving advice to his son on the proper way to govern. The old king reaffirms the traditional doctrine that only character and moral life endure and insures one's memory among the people. He says: *"Remember, more acceptable is the virtue of an upright man than the ox of him that doeth iniquity."* Kingship, he reminds his son, is rooted not in power, but in justice. Thus, *"do righteousness that thou mayest be established on earth."* The old man warns his son that he must actively seek to do good. *"Comfort the mourner....afflict not the widow...deprive not a man of the possessions of his father...do not chastise...slay not a man whose worth thou knowest...Be not harsh, kindness is seemly...establish thy monument in the love of thee."* (38) All of this is traditional Egyptian moral thinking as far as it goes. But when Merikere warns his son that *"god knoweth the rebellious man and god smiteth his iniquity in blood,"* he is giving voice to the new importance afforded the idea of judgement after death and its relevance to moral behavior on earth.

Whereas Ptahotep had warned that doing right in this world was good in itself because it formed good character, Merikere has taken the argument one step further. In terrible times justice and reward in this life are uncertain. It is the age old problem that later perplexed both Christians and Jews of how to insure that the good are somehow rewarded when it is obvious that they are often not rewarded in this life. Merikere turns to the old idea of a final judgement and links it to the proper behavior of a king.

> *"The court of the judges who judge the unworthy, thou knowest that* counter consequential
>
> *they are not lenient on that day of judging the wretched, in the*
>
> *hour of executing the writ....A man surviveth after death and his*
>
> *deeds are placed beside him like mountains. For it is eternity, abiding*
>
> *yonder, a fool is he who disregards it. As for him who reacheth it*
>
> *without having committed sin, he shall abide there like a god, striding*
>
> *on like the lords of eternity."* (39)

Character remains something good in itself. But now it is also part of man's personal relationship with his god and plays a part in the manner in which man achieves a proper judgement after death.

This is a shift in value between god and man. No longer is it merely the externals of life that matter, for in difficult times they are uncertain in any case. Merikere is saying that the value of a worthy moral life includes the expectation that god will reward it after death. It is a desperate faith, born of the harsh experience of internecine strife with its encompassing uncertainty. In these circumstances character and conscience become the currency of a person's moral worth, and every person had a conscience. It was the beginning of an age of ethical democratization, of the idea that Everyman could aspire to eternal reward and fair judgement.

The genuine despair that accompanied the collapse of Egyptian society is captured poignantly in a text entitled *The Dialogue of A Misanthrope With His Own Soul*. It is one of the most famous and important poems in Egyptian literature because its theme is unique. The subject is the inner experience of an afflicted and suffering soul, the first example in history of the self-examined conscience as a state of mind, (40) and the earliest known literary composition in which the subject is spiritual experience. It is the Egyptian equivalent of the *Book of Job* written fifteen hundred years earlier. (41) The *Dialogue* is the tale of a man against whom all circumstances have turned. Deep in his own darkness and despair, he decides to take his own life. He stands on the edge of his grave looking down and begins a conversation with his reluctant soul who refuses to accompany him into the shadows. It is history's first dialogue with the self, Freudian in our terms, dark and suffering. The Misanthrope's words tell of a society that is corrupt, dishonest, and unjust. So terrible has life in Egypt become that the sufferer despairs of an honest judgment beyond the grave. The sufferer's soul at first refuses to join him in death forcing him to contemplate the joys of material life. But it is no use. The contemplation only strengthens the suffer's conviction that this life is without worth. Finding only small faith in the promise of redemption beyond the grave, the sufferer embraces death as a welcome release. The unhappy man's soul finally relents and both pass into the shadow of death. (42)

The *Dialogue* centers upon the human experience of the sufferer and does not mention god as either cause or cure of human misery. It is an example of an emerging literature concerned for the first time with self-examination and self-awareness. (43) We are witnessing the evolution of a self-awareness that recognizes the individual as a moral force in *social* life. All the suffering is condemned precisely because it afflicts individuals. The moral unworthiness of the society is located in the injustices it visits upon people and not just because it displeases god. The moral thinkers of the Feudal Age have realized that the connection between moral character and the social conditions which confront the individual attempting to live a moral life has been broken. The new task is to reestablish it.

The *Song of the Harp-Player* is a hymn inscribed on the tomb of a king dating from around 2100 B.C.E. that also richly captures the skepticism and disillusionment that followed the end of the Pyramid Age. The author demonstrates how empty and insufficient wealth and power are as vehicles for the attainment of happiness and heaven. The author admonishes us to work to develop good character and morals in all spheres of life. The *Song of the Harp-Player* is a study in reflective morals that asks what is necessary for a man to be made good and to gain salvation. The idea of looking within for the answer is as old as the *Memphite Drama*. But now the area of moral concern has moved beyond the individual to a skeptical detachment through which ethical concerns may go beyond the self to include the social order. The same theme is found in the treatise of Khekheperre-sonbu, a priest at Heliopolis during the reign of Sesostris II (1906-1887 B.C.E.). The author speaks of his deep personal despair, but goes on to make a striking moral critique of the society in which he lives. Taken together both these works point to the emergence of Egyptian moralists' clear concern with social justice. The time of troubles has forced ethical thinkers to extend their range of topics beyond the individual to include man's relationship with his god and the relationship of both to the justice or injustice of the social order.

Probably the most remarkable document of the period is the *Admonition of Ipuwer*, although its date is uncertain. (44) True to Egyptian literary form, the dissertation is cast in the form of a discussion between a wise man (Ipuwer) and the king himself (perhaps Pepy II). Ipuwer begins with a long description of the ills which bedevil Egyptian society including a discussion of the evils that are permitted to exist. He argues that these wrongs exist because of the moral failures of important officials whom the king has failed to adequately control. The remedy for these injustices, Ipuwer asserts, is a proper king who possesses certain character and behavioral habits which Ipuwer then enumerates in great detail. The *Admonition of Ipuwer* may be regarded as the first treatise on political ethics in history. For the first time someone is asking the question, in what does a good state consist?

No less startling is Ipuwer's solution for the curse of an unjust political order. Like Plato and Thomas Aquinas, Ipuwer suggests that reform and justice can be brought about by a great king who seeks justice by right action. But where is such a king to be found, Ipuwer asks. *"Where is he today? Doth he sleep perchance? Behold his might is not yet seen...as yet."* It is unclear if Ipuwer intends this question as a subtle threat of revolution against the sitting king or if it is the first expression of politico-religious messianism fifteen hundred years before the idea of a king who rules by god's wishes for justice appeared among the Israelites. (45) In either case, the substance of Ipuwer's argument is clear: injustice is caused by bad kings and only good kings who do god's wishes (*Maat*) can restore justice. Like Nathan's famous accusation of King David, "thou art the man," Ipuwer's *Admonition* places the responsibility for the just society squarely on the shoulders of the sovereign. Ipuwer shows a new Egyptian capacity to contemplate society in terms of its moral soundness. But it is the ability to move beyond contemplation and suggest mechanisms of reform that is revolutionary. This Egyptian writer, perhaps as early as the Sixth Dynasty, produced a dissertation much like the *Republic*, seeking to determine the qualities necessary for a just civic order and placing the responsibility for their achievement squarely upon the ruler.

The wisdom texts of the Feudal Age reveal the new way in which Egyptians had come to think about morals and ethics. Strength of character and conscience were now thought of as something more than the value they possess for influencing individual conduct. They have now become a moral force incorporating concerns about what happens to other men and even to society itself. Pleading good character is no longer enough. Human beings and social institutions must always *do* what is right or be held responsible for their failure. This thinking was a reaction to the uncertainty of the times, and it inevitably raised questions about the state and the behavior of the king and his officials. The result was a literature quite specific about how to form a good state and what qualities and actions a king had to possess in order to do justice. No one believed, of course, that a bad king could be brought to book on this earth. But the king could be called to account beyond the grave for his unjust actions, and the penalties were just as severe for him as for any man.

The age-old ideal that the king and the powerful must practice *Maat* now took on new importance, and this was reflected in the tomb and coffin inscriptions of nobles and government officials. (46) These inscriptions reflect a new urgency to do good as the necessary prerequisite for a positive judgement after death. By the Middle Kingdom (2040-1674 B.C.E.) the ethical conduct of public officials has come to be regarded as the only way in which just government can be properly achieved. Egypt has arrived at a point in its history where it expects ethical rulers, officials, and laws as the normative ideal to implement the command of god to pursue social justice. It would be another thousand years before any other people, first among them the Israelites, would see government in this way.

The democratization of the Osiris myth that had begun at the beginning of the Feudal Age reached full development during the Middle Kingdom. The linkage between social justice and religion extant in the command of the god to do justice and the responsibility of the king to see that justice is done produced important changes in the Osiran faith. The gods were now seen as the origin and followers of *Maat,* and gradually come to assume the role of the protectors of the poor and powerless. Osiris emerges during this period as the unmistakable champion of righteousness, standing side-by-side with Re in the official theology of the age. God made all men equal in the moral sense so that all must be judged by

Osiris after death. The doctrine of final judgement, once exclusively reserved for Egypt's kings, now extends to the common man. Osiris has become Everyman. The coffin texts of the period reflect the idea that all humans are morally equal. The following inscriptions are typical of the period.

> *"I have made the four winds so that every man might breathe thereof like his brother."*

> *"I have made the great waters that the pauper like the lord might have use of them."*

> *"I have made everyman like his brother, and I have forbidden that they do evil..."* (47)

The Osiris theology democratized the moral value of men by making them equal in the eyes of god. This implied that all were equal when it came to the opportunity for a final judgement and eternal life. This is an extraordinary development in ethical history, but one that occurs within the mainstream of Egyptian ethical thought which had always affirmed that all men had the moral responsibility to do *Maat*. Now they are granted equal treatment in the hereafter precisely because they possessed equal moral worth and responsibility. These ideas strengthened the old Egyptian belief that all persons stood equal before the law. What is remarkable about this democratization of morals and law is that it occurs at the same time that King Hammurabi of Babylon promulgated his famous Code. The contrast between Egyptian and Babylonian concepts of law could not be more striking. Hammurabi's code affirmed no equality under the law, nor did it offer an ethical basis for punishment. Law and punishment followed social class and position, functions of royal power without ethical content. In Egypt it is precisely the ethical equality of men in the eyes of god that requires their equal treatment under the law. And it is precisely the moral injunction of god to do justice that forms the foundation of proportional punishment within the law.

The development of Egyptian ethical thinking continued until the end of the Imperial Age almost a thousand years later. During the magnificent 18th Dynasty (1552-1069 B.C.E.), Egypt rose to become a world power spreading its influence, knowledge, culture, and religion throughout the Near East. The powerful local god of Thebes, Amun, arose to take his place within the great trinity of Re, Osiris, and Amun. The depth and influence of Egyptian ethical tradition is demonstrated by the fact that this local Theban-war god quickly assumed the same ethical qualities and duties of the other gods. Amun became the helper of the poor, the protector of the weak, a loving father, and an incorruptible judge who treated rich and poor alike. (48) The loving character of the new imperial god is reflected in his official hymn where he is described as the "Lord of Life." Men seek comfort from him for *"my heart has no other refuge than Amun"* and when *"Amen-Re is the strength of the lonely."* (49) Amun is the father who cares for his children. His hymn says of him *"He who heareth the prayer of the prisoner; kindly of heart when one calleth to him. He who rescueth the fearful from the oppressor, who judgeth between the miserable and the strong."* (50) There can be no more convincing testimony to the influence of the Egyptian ethical tradition on Egyptian life and politics than this simple fact: the god of the Egyptian imperium in whose name Egypt conquered the region is at one and the same time a just and loving god who sees to the just treatment of his people. It is a god that stands in marked contrast to the savage god of the Israelites who is about to make his appearance on the stage of history.

The presence of a loving and just god who promised fair judgement and immortality had a dramatic effect on ethics in that it increased the growing awareness of man's personal relationship with his god and an awareness of his personal responsibility for moral behavior. When Egyptians reflected on ethics they turned increasingly inward listening closely to the voice of moral intuition within their hearts. Moral thinkers came to understand that man's moral responsibility depended upon his own conscious understanding of himself and his god. Men now had to make moral decisions according to the inner voices of their consciences. Here is the first evidence in history of man recognizing the role of conscience in ethical reasoning, an idea that came eventually to occupy a central place in later Western ideas of ethics. The Egyptian ethical sense had become quasi-secular by the end of the Middle Kingdom and was more closely tied to the idea of an afterlife and final judgement than at any time previously. Following the Imperial Age (1552-1188 B.C.E.), or the New Kingdom as it is often called, the ideal of conscience took on a new dimension in which personal piety came to play an important role in moral behavior.

The great insights that Egyptian thinkers had reached in ethics, morals, and religion had until now remained concealed from the world. Except for the period of the Hyksos invasion and occupation (1674-1552 B.C.E.), Egypt had remained sealed behind her geographical barriers for almost 2500 years! Her contacts with other societies of her time were minimal and produced no lasting effect on the direction of her own development. Egyptian ideas of morality and religion were completely her own, developed and applied over many centuries entirely within an Egyptian context. By the sixteenth century B.C.E., Egypt was poised by force of arms to expel the Hyksos invaders and to carry Egyptian power throughout the

Middle East. The great Imperial Age, the time of the Warrior Pharaohs, was about to begin. Egypt's great culture would now be set loose upon the world. Neither Egypt nor the world would ever be the same.

The new universal god of Egypt possessed all the characteristics that Egyptian religious thought had attributed to its former gods, including a concern for ethics and justice. The universal god was not a conquering national warrior god like the god of the Israelites. Nor was it the "enclave god" of the Canaanites, a god whose wrath and wisdom applied only to the tribe. Re-Amun was a universal deity whose task it was to make certain men lived according to justice. The kind, caring, and just god that the Egyptian theologians of the Feudal Age had fashioned for themselves became universalized under the New Kingdom. And a universal god of justice inevitably became the only god.

NOTES

1. James H. Breasted, *The Dawn of Conscience* (New York: Charles Scribner, 1947.

2. Breasted, 24.

3. Rosalie David, *The Ancient Egyptians: Religious Beliefs and Practices* (London: Routledge and Kegan Paul, 1982), 14.

4. Breasted, 18.

5. E.A. Wallis Budge, *From Fetish to God in Ancient Egypt* (New York: Dover Publications, 1988), 263.

6. Breasted, 35.

7. *The New American Bible* (New York: Catholic Book Publishing House, 1992), see Section II, The Gospel of St. John, 144.

8. Budge, vi.

9. Jan Assmann, *Moses the Egyptian* (Cambridge, MA: Harvard University Press, 1997), 195.

10. Ibid.

11. Siegfried Morenz, *Egyptian Religion* (Ithaca, NY: Cornell University Press, 1973), 143.

12. Ibid., 142.

13. Ibid., 140.

14. Ibid., 142. The use of the singular in this way is called the "majestic singular."

15. Ibid., 143.

16. Ibid., 273.

17. Breasted, 129.

18. David, 19.

19. *Everyday Life Through the Ages* (London: Readers' Digest Association Ltd., 1992), 28.

20. Morenz, 125.

21. Ibid., 119.

22. For an account of Yahweh's rampages against his people during the Mosaic period, see Jonathan Kirsch, *Moses: A Life* (New York: Ballantine Books, 1998).

23. Morenz, 132.

24. The Egyptian idea of man's ethical obligation as caretaker of his environment and the animals he shares it with stands in stark contrast to the Israelite and Christian view that god granted man "dominion" over the things of the earth.

25. Morenz, 124.

26. Breasted, 45.

27. Karen Armstrong, *A History of God* (New York: Ballantine Books, 1993), 18.

28. David, 33. Just when cannibalism may have been practiced in Egypt is uncertain, but no doubt it was before predynastic times and, most likely, even before the Mesopotamian influence. To the south, however, in the Sudan, it is likely that this practice, along with secondary burial, continued until more recent times.

29. Breasted, 87.

30. In portraying the soul in art, Christians often showed it as a nude infant emerging from the mouth of the deceased as it rose toward heaven.

31. Breasted, 48.

32. Rosalie David, *The Cult of the Sun: Myth and Magic in Ancient Egypt* (New York: Barnes and Noble, 1998), 160.

33. Breasted, 97.

34. Budge, 265-266.

35. Morenz, 131.

36. David, *The Cult of the Sun*, 46.

37. Sir Alan Gardiner, *Egypt of the Pharaohs* (London: Oxford University Press, 1961), 105-106.

38. Breasted, 154.

39. Ibid. 157.

40. David, *The Cult of the Sun*, 123.

41. Breasted, 169.

42. Ibid., 171-176 for the complete text of the *Dialogue*.

43. David, *The Cult of the Sun*, 123.

44. David places the *Admonition* in the Sixth Dynasty while Breasted dates it considerably more recently.

45. James H. Breasted, *Development of Religion and Thought in Ancient Egypt* (New York: Harper and Brothers, 1959), 210-213. This is an important book, first published in 1912. All subsequent studies of Egyptian religion and thought are indebted to Breasted's original study.

46. During the Middle Kingdom when the cedar coffin came into wide use, the old pyramid texts were inscribed on the inside of the coffins. These texts were changed to be more relevant to the common populace as the original pyramid texts were designed to be used by the king and the nobility. Production of these coffin texts became lucrative business for the temples, and they were written

down as scrolls to be interred with the dead. These scrolls came to be known as the *Book of the Dead*. It should be noted, however, that there was no such book (and it is not the "Bible of the Egyptians!). Whatever scrolls were interred depended upon the sales ability of the priests. There is no formal and complete collection that could reasonably be called a "book."

47. Breasted, *The Dawn of Conscience*, 299.

48. David, *The Cult of the Sun*, 183.

49. Donald B. Redford, *Akhenaten: The Heretic King* (Princeton, NJ: Princeton University Press, 1984), 178.

50. Assmann, 181.

2

The Egyptian Origins of Christianity

The search for the Egyptian origins of Christianity begins with an examination of the traditional Egyptian religious beliefs that prevailed in Egypt for more than three thousand years before being displaced by Christianity sometime in the second century of the Common Era. The question to be examined is whether or not these traditional Egyptian theological beliefs can be found to characterize Christianity, if only in part. If a reasonably convincing argument can be made to explain the similarity in fundamental theological beliefs between Christianity and Egyptian theology, we may conclude that Christianity is *not* a genuinely new theological system but a *newly expressed* form of a far older theological system whose origins lay within Egyptian history and culture.

Egyptian theology was characterized from antiquity by three elements: (1) a monotheistic belief in a deity who manifested his power in the sun and its operations; (2) the cult of the regenerating power of nature expressed in the adoration of ithyphallic gods and animals; and (3) a perception of anthropomorphic divinity where the life of man continues beyond death in the celebration of an afterlife.(1) These themes were fully articulated by the 5th Dynasty (2500 B.C.E.) where they can be found inscribed in tombs and on monuments. It is a reasonable assumption that Egyptians were thinking and writing about these theological themes for a very long time, perhaps even a millennium, before written evidence of their existence was preserved. One does not, after all, arrive at such sophisticated ideas overnight. Their development requires considerable intellectual spadework before anything approaching a comprehensive formulation is possible. Monotheism, regeneration, and immortality are not simple ideas.

The development of a conceptual vocabulary to express such ideas is itself a remarkable achievement, and Egyptian theologians were the first in history to invent and use a conceptual vocabulary. Early in the 20th century C.E. it was thought that the Egyptian language as expressed in hieroglyphs was too literal to permit the development of abstract terms. Writing in 1914, Gardiner argued that the Egyptians were not "philosophical" in that they did not manipulate abstract terms. (2) As with so much about Egypt, this conclusion was based upon partial knowledge of the artifact under examination. The language of Egyptian theologians was indeed sufficiently abstract and they arrived at such highly abstract ideas as incarnation, the soul, the beatification of the body, a complete psychology of the human person, a psychology of the dead, notions of political and social justice, the unity behind the complexity of being, a trinitarian god, and the distinction between substance and accident, to mention but a few. Egyptian semantics recognized the difference between abstract and descriptive terms by requiring that a hieroglyphic descriptive be inserted at the end a word group whenever the meaning intended was abstract. Egyptian scholars inserted the hieroglyph of a rolled papyrus scroll to indicate that the thing expressed was a product of the mind and not something that could be found outside the mind. (3) Equipped with a vocabulary to express abstract concepts of their own invention, Egyptian theologians became the first humans in history to manipulate and express complex abstract ideas and to write them down in stone and on papyrus for discovery by future generations.

The fundamental features of Egyptian religion remained unchanged in their essentials from the 5th Dynasty down to the period when Egypt began to embrace Christianity around 69 C.E. (4) This endurance did not prevent the main theological principles from being more completely refined and articulated, a process that led to significant changes in the manner in which theological fundamentals were understood. But from beginning to end, Egyptian religion remained centered upon the following principles: (1) a single trinitarian god; (2) a cosmology in which all things, man, god, and nature, have a place that can be comprehended by man; (3) man's possession of an immortal soul; (4) resurrection of the dead; (5) a final judgement beyond the grave where man's ethical life is weighed; and (6) an eternal life for the virtuous. These principles continued to characterize Egyptian theology from its beginning until its destruction in the fourth century of the Common Era.

I have already explored the first two theological principles in some detail in the previous chapter. It need only be recalled here that over the centuries the original solar monotheism of the Egyptians gradually transformed itself into a monotheism where the single god was expressed as a trinitarian entity in which all three persons were present, distinct, and equally divine. Over the centuries the single god changed from an Egyptian national god to a universal deity "who watcheth over the earth hourly," one concerned with all humanity everywhere. The other Egyptian principle of a natural order encompassing all things permitted the development of a moral cosmology where all beings were required to do *Maat*, that is justice or that which is appropriate to the thing's nature. This principle explained the place of man and god in the universe. God himself must pursue *Maat*, a principle that early on transformed the Egyptian god into a just and loving god. Thus it was that when the Persians conquered Egypt in 525 B.C.E., followed by Alexander and the Greeks in 332 B.C.E., and then by the Romans in 31 B.C.E., all three cultures encountered a deity whose character none had encountered before. Only in Palestine, and then not before the 5th century B.C.E., does one find another people of the ancient world beginning to think of their god as genuinely monotheistic, merciful, and just. These people were the Jews. Over more than seven hundred years their early Mosaic theology had transformed itself into a truly monotheistic, ethically casuistic one that affirmed a universal god of justice and mercy.

The principles of Egyptian theology were all derived from the incorporation of the Osiris myth into the body of traditional Egyptian religious thought, a process that began even before the First Union (3200 B.C.E.), although the first available written evidence dates from the 5th Dynasty (2500 B.C.E.). It is very probable that the cult of the dead and the accompanying idea of an afterlife originated even before the dawn of the 4th millennium. (5) The legend of Osiris became so thoroughly integrated into Egyptian theology that it transformed the solar Re mythology to promise resurrection and life after death for the individual believer regardless of rank or station, a privilege that the original solar theology had reserved previously to the king and the powerful. Over two thousand years the central solar myth of Egyptian theology became "Osirized" in that the justification for and the character of the king's resurrection became expressed entirely in terms of the Osiris myth. So close was the identification of the king's resurrection with the Osiris myth that when the king rose again after death he was said *to become* Osiris. (6) The first written evidence of the adoption of Osiris into the solar myth appeared during the Pyramid Age. By the end of that period the importance of Osiris in the solar myth of divine resurrection of the king was reflected in the incorporation of Osiris into the company of the four solar genii known as the Four Eastern Horuses. (7) These genii accompanied the king into the afterlife, and for the first time Osiris was listed among them, signifying that in the official theology of the resurrection of the king Osiris was recognized as playing an important role.

Once the Osiris myth asserted its importance within the state solar theology, it was only a matter of time before it would spread to the rest of the populace. The great attraction of the Osiris myth was its promise of life after death. By the end of the Feudal Age Osiris had achieved a place equal to Re in the faith of the common man creating a theological duality within the Egyptian religious tradition. The official religion of the king and the state remained the solar myth of Re even as it absorbed the premises of the Osiris myth into the official theology. The Osiris myth spread among the general populace and gradually developed an institutional structure of its own. The syncretic nature of Egyptian religion prevented conflict between the two myths, and Osiris gradually became solarized while Re became Osirized into a single complete theology. This syncretism was already evident during the Feudal Age, but became more formally so by the New Kingdom where the need of Egyptian theologians to accommodate the desires of the warrior pharaohs to raise their local god, Amun, to national status led them to reemphasize the trinitarian nature of the single god and create the trinity of Re, Osiris, and Amun.

The official incorporation of the Osiris myth into the Egyptian religious tradition and its wide support among the Egyptian population led to the doctrine of resurrection becoming the central theological principle of Egyptian religion that was transmitted to the West through the Greek and Roman occupations of Egypt. This is in itself an amazing fact. Here we find a doctrine of eternal life and the resurrection of a glorified body based upon an ancient story of the resurrection of Oriris after suffering a cruel and horrible death inflicted by the powers of evil that is at least four thousand years old and unchanged in its essentials throughout all periods of Egyptian history before being transmitted to the West. The Osiris theology of resurrection and eternal life became more widespread and of greater theological influence in the Hellenistic and Roman periods than at any other time in its theological history. (8)

The Egyptians believed in a life beyond the grave from very earliest times and the doctrine of eternal existence became a leading feature of their religious history. It was an idea that greatly affected Egyptian thinking about ethics, for if life was possible beyond the grave, then the question of who was to be saved and how became a central moral question. Breasted rightly claimed that "among no people, ancient or modern, has the idea of a life beyond the grave held so prominent a place as among ancient Egyptians." (9) He may have added that the ideas of resurrection and eternal life were unique to Egypt and did not appear in any other ancient culture until the first century of the Common Era.

Osiris was one of the oldest gods of Egypt, perhaps as ancient as Re himself, although Osiris' role as god of the dead evolved much later. The two most obvious elements in ancient Egyptian life were the sun and the Nile and both, albeit in different forms, came to be venerated as gods. Re personified the sun while Osiris came to represent the everlasting cycles of vegetation where plants grow, reproduce, and die to be renewed by the waters of the Nile each year and restored to life again. It is likely that Osiris may have his earliest origins as a god of vegetation. (10) Because the agricultural cycles were familiar to all Egyptians, Osiris' behavior, like the plants of the Nile, was also familiar. Osiris was never a remote god in the sense that Re was. From the beginning Osiris was involved in human affairs.

There was, however, another side to Osiris which may have had its roots in distant historical events. In pre-dynastic times, well before the First Union, Osiris was already regarded as the god of the dead. With the myth of the afterlife not yet fully developed, death was to be feared and the god that presided over it to be feared as well. There were very ancient spells and charms whose power it was to protect the living from the god of the dead. The roots of this fear are very ancient. There is a legend, predating the First Dynasty, that speaks of a man who rose from the dead and made himself lord of the dead. We are wholly ignorant of who this person was, but he was known for thousands of years to the Egyptians as *Khenti-Amenti*, or He Who is Chief of the Amenti. Later this legend became associated with Osiris, but we do not know for what reasons. (11) There is another legend that attributes to Osiris the outlawing of cannibalism among the Egyptians. Cannibalism, mostly of the ritual variety where one consumes some part of another person to gain for oneself the best qualities of the deceased, was an old custom in Africa and at some time in the pre-dynastic past may have been practiced by the Egyptians. A text in the tomb of Pharaoh Unas of the 5th Dynasty (2500 B.C.E.) tells of a time when the chief god hunted down the lesser gods to kill, cook, and eat them, which leads Budge to conclude that the Egyptians practiced cannibalism perhaps much later than we would have expected. (12)

The story of Osiris' death rings of cannibalism. After Osiris was murdered his body was mutilated, his genitals cut off, his organs and bones scattered, and his head severed and buried in a secret place. It is possible, Budge theorizes, that this was a common practice in Egypt before the arrival of the pre-dynastic race whose influence shaped early Egyptian culture. If the king of these foreigners outlawed the practice, the memory of his doing so might have remained as a vague folk tale of the god who prohibited the terrible practice and required the intact burial of the dead. (13) While the legend has a sense of plausibility about it, it seems to me that whatever may have been prohibited by this early king, it was probably not cannibalism. The description of Osiris' death preserved in his myth is more probably a description of the common practice, still extant in Africa, of second-burial where the deceased is placed in the ground for several months until the soft tissues of the body decay. The body is then disinterred. The remaining flesh is scraped from the skeleton and the bones and skull given to the deceased's relatives or important persons of the tribe who valued them as tokens of the deceased's virtue or strength. Second-burial was far more likely to have been practiced in Upper Egypt where the moist soil of the Delta lands encouraged rapid decay of the body. In the desert regions of Lower Egypt, it is far more likely that burial in the desert sands would have produced mummification.

If, as some historians believe, Osiris was an actual king of some powerful city of Lower Egypt who defeated a king of a Delta city, it is not unlikely that he would have been appalled at the practice of second-burial and outlawed it. In which case he might have ordered that henceforth all bodies were to be interred intact and, as was likely the custom of his native Lower Egypt, that the intact corpse was to be buried in the hot desert sands at the edge of the Nile. Under these conditions natural desiccation of the bodies would have occurred and Egyptians would have come across corpses whose desiccated bodies looked remarkably as they did in life. Breasted suggests that it was this natural mummification that might have given rise to the idea of life beyond the grave. (14)

The Egyptian emphasis upon preserving the corpse, however it began, was soon absorbed into Egyptian theology with important consequences. Egypt's early kings labored mightily to construct their tombs with the sole objective of preserving their bodies for all eternity. The idea took root that eternal life could only be preserved as long as the earthly body remained intact in the tomb. The preservation of the body became central to Egyptian theology even though within that theology there was no explanation of why the body had to be preserved. The injunction to preserve the body rings of a royal command more than a theological argument, perhaps the original command of Osiris himself as a real king. It might also be that Osiris's forbidding of second-burial (or cannibalism if Budge is right) resulted in the preservation of the deceased through natural desiccation almost as an accidental consequence. If, when the real Osiris died, he was buried in the manner of his native region, that is, in the desert sand where his body might become naturally mummified, the king's manner of burial may have been widely adopted or even commanded to be so. What began as a royal edict became associated with the burial habits of the king who was thought to be divine from the earliest times so that they became associated with the burial of gods. When the early priests tried to make theological sense of the practice it was but a short step to the idea that the body of a god had to be preserved to enjoy the afterlife.

This is, of course, speculation. What seems less speculative, however, is the attribution of great acts of violence to Osiris as he appeared in his earliest iterations. Chapter 28 of the *Book of the Dead* tells of a great battle which took place at night between the forces of Osiris and the Sebau fiends who were associates of Set. Osiris ordered all the prisoners to be butchered. In another paragraph the story tells of a night when Osiris sat in judgement of prisoners. He ordered the good separated from the wicked and pronounced a sentence of doom upon the latter. The condemned were beheaded, their bodies cut to pieces and burned. Their spirits and souls were severed from their bodies and their shadows driven away. The skulls of the condemned were battered in and pieces of bone cast down into a pit of fire. (15) In these old legends Osiris was always accompanied by *Shesmu*, his chief executioner. (16) What makes these legends real is that later pharaohs did much the same thing to their enemies. Beginning with Narmer, almost every pharaoh was portrayed on his monuments slaughtering his enemies with abandon. A common title associated with these portrayals was "Shatterer of Skulls." It might be that the legend of Osiris had its roots in some historical dynastic struggle that occurred in pre-dynastic times leaving only faint echoes to reach the modern ear.

Christine Hobson argues strongly for the view that the Osiris myth has historical roots. She notes that in pre-dynastic times there were few major cities along the Nile. One of these cities was Nubt (near modern Naqada), whose priesthood was dedicated to the local god Seth. Nubt was an ideal marketing center standing on the Nile bank near Wadi Hammamat, one of the few routes across the eastern desert and the main road to the gold fields. The other town located south of modern Luxor was the town of Nekhen (modern El Kab). Its local god was the falcon or Horus, a fact that gave rise much later to the Greeks calling it Hieraconpolis or Falcon City. (17) The ancient story of the battle between Horus and Seth that was folded into the Osiris myth was probably a folk memory of a war between these two cities. The victory of Horus over Seth, that is of Hieraconpolis over Nubt, gave the former authority over all of Upper Egypt as well as southward to the Nubian border. (18) Further evidence suggests that the attempt to establish a common administration and a common irrigation system led to the conquest of all Egypt by Menes. Having brought the country under his authority, Narmer established a new capital at the neck of the Delta and the Nile Valley. Originally called *Inbuhed* or City of the White Walls for its whitewashed defensive fortifications, the city later became known as *Mennefer* which the Greeks called Memphis. (19) It remained the capitol of the country on and off for more than three thousand years.

By the time the two countries of Upper and Lower Egypt were united under one king (3400 B.C.E.), Osiris had lost much of his fearful quality as a god of the dead and slaughterer of the wicked. He became the god that pharaoh looked to guide him into the paradise of eternal life. At this early date the idea that Osiris might guide the common man to the same destination was still beyond comprehension. Within a few centuries Osiris became identified with the eternal fate of pharaoh himself. Osiris' importance in the Egyptian pantheon was evident in his incorporation into the oldest religious festival in Egyptian history, the *Heb-Sed*. (20) During the ceremony pharaoh impersonated Osiris by assuming the costume of the god thereby beginning the process of incorporating Osiris into the solar theology of Re himself. It would be many centuries before Osiris would eclipse the influence of Re and bring to the world the solace of the new doctrine that the common man could overcome death. But the idea had already begun to take root in the consciousness of Egyptian theologians at a very early date.

The story of Osiris, his death, resurrection, and reward of eternal life has all the characteristics of a dynastic struggle with historical roots that was later infused with theological substance. The legend begins with a conflict between two brothers, Osiris and Set, who because they were kings or, perhaps, aspirants to the same throne, were regarded as sons of god who had taken on a human nature upon their birth, an idea that later pharaohs adopted to explain their own divine origins. The divine Osiris became man and suffered a human destiny by becoming mortal. (21) He endured evil, torment, and death as the experience of his humanity, and became the only Egyptian god to suffer death and rise again from it, events that make him very different from all the other gods of ancient Egypt. (22) The parallel with the Christian doctrine concerning Jesus' human nature and incarnation is obvious, but must remain unexplored for the moment.

Osiris was married to Isis who was also his sister while Set was married to Isis' sister, Nephthys, who was also his sister. This reflects the very ancient practice of the early kings of Egypt marrying their sisters as a way to preserve the blood lineage of the nobility. This practice was probably introduced by the pre-dynastic race that arrived in Egypt before the 4th millennium. For reasons that are not clear, Set grew envious of Osiris and murdered him. Here again is a hint of a dynastic struggle between two brothers.

In one version of the myth Osiris was locked in a trunk, drowned, and taken to Nedyt, possibly the area around Byblos in Lebanon, where he was buried in a secret place. In another version that became the more commonly accepted one

Set mutilated the body of Osiris, chopping it into pieces and scattering it throughout Egypt. In this version Osiris or only his head was buried at Abydos, which later became the most sacred shrine to Osiris. Abydos has been venerated from very ancient times as one of the most sacred places in Egypt. It was here on the wide desert plain that the first kings of Egypt were buried, among them all the kings of the First Dynasty and two of the Second. Surrounded by small stone tombs containing the bodies of servants, dwarfs, women, and other retainers are the graves of Narmer, Aha, Djer, Merneith, Djet, Den Adjib, Smerkhe, and Qa'a, Egypt's earliest and most venerated sovereigns. (23) Since Egyptians believed that the legend of Osiris referred to a real king, one of the ancient tombs was believed to be Osiris' burial place. (24)

By the Middle Kingdom Abydos had assumed the status of Egypt's most sacred place. Powerful nobles wished to be buried there, and it became common practice for the less wealthy to have their mummified bodies transported to the city for a special blessing before returning them to a more local burial place. Every year thousands of pilgrims visited the sacred site, and each year a grand drama portraying the death and resurrection of Osiris was staged to enormous crowds. In stature and sanctity the burial site of Osiris at Abydos was equivalent to the Church of the Holy Sepulchre in Jerusalem.

When news of Osiris' death reached Isis, she and her sister began to search for his body. The two searched the world bringing together each piece of Osiris' body as they found it. With the help of Anubis sent by the sun god, the two sisters embalmed Osiris' body, assembling the pieces by wrapping them in bandages. Here is the first description of the preservation of a corpse by human action instead of by natural desiccation, a practice which legend tells us was begun with Osiris. (25) From this time forward Osiris was always portrayed as a wrapped mummy. But even in death the life-giving power of Osiris could not be destroyed, and Isis mated with the corpse of her husband. The description of their coupling is dramatic. *"Isis drew near her husband and making a shadow with her pinions and causing a wind to change with her wings…raising the weary limbs of the silent-hearted* (the deceased Osiris), *receiving his seed, bringing forth an heir, nursing the child in solitude, whose place is not known, introducing him when his arms grew strong to the Great Hall of the gods at Heliopolis."* (26)

The child that resulted from this union was Horus. When Set learns about the child he knows that Horus will someday attempt to revenge his father. Set sets out to kill Horus. Isis hid in the reeds and swamps of the Nile Delta where she nursed and raised her son. Portrayals of Isis holding the baby Horus were common images in Egypt for millennia, and their resemblance to the Christian images of Madonna and Child are striking. Isis and Horus survived many adventures as Set attempted several times to murder the child. One of the most poignant events occurred when Set convinced the scorpion god to sting the child. Horus was stung and lingered near death. Isis petitioned the gods to save her son. Portrayed in Egyptian art, Isis holds the limp body of her suffering divine son who hovers near death, an image similar to that expressed by Michelangelo in his famous *Pieta*. But the gods intervened and Horus recovered. (27) Grown to manhood "when his arm is strong" Horus seeks out and does combat with Set to avenge the death of Osiris. It is a fierce fight in which Horus loses his eye. But in the end Set is defeated. Horus's eye is returned to him by Toth. Horus returns to Abydos and the grave of his father.

Horus offered his eye to his father as a token of filial devotion. From this day forward the eye of Horus cast in stone or metal became the most popular amulet among Egyptians. Because of Horus' devotion to his father, the gods gathered around Osiris' grave and there was wailing and crying out. With the help of Anubis, the jackal god of embalmers, and the formulae repeated by Toth, the god of knowledge, Horus performed the ceremony of resurrection, the first expression of that radical idea in the history of mankind! The Osiran myth describes the great moment: *"Horus comes to thee, he separates thy bandages, he throws off thy bonds. Arise, give thou thy hand to Horus, that he may raise thee up. The tomb is opened for him. The bricks are drawn for thee out of the great tomb..."* And then, *"Osiris awakes, the weary god wakens, the god stands up, he gains control of his body. Stand up! Thou shalt not end, thou shalt not perish."* (28) Osiris rises from the dead and the new idea of resurrection is given its first expression in human terms. Ever since that time mankind has continued to hope that, like Osiris, we too might triumph over death.

Despite his defeat at the hands of Horus, Set refuses to relinquish his cause and brings charges against Horus and Osiris to be heard by the gods sitting in the Great Hall of Heliopolis. The legend does not reveal the charges, but it is most likely that Set is challenging Horus' claim to the kingdom on the grounds that he is illegitimate, for surely Osiris was dead when Horus was conceived. Isis, therefore, has produced a pretender to the throne or she is a common harlot. (29) Once more the story resembles the tale of a dynastic struggle, this time based on the legitimacy of blood lineage. The assembly of the gods that heard the case in the Great Hall resembled a meeting of powerful nobles or even kings called to decide the merits of the rival claimants. That such an assemblage of nobles should be thought of as gods is not unusual. In the early days of Rome, the assembly of the ruling families was commonly thought to be an assembling of the gods. The gods ruled in favor of Osiris declaring him to be *maet kheru*, that is, "true of word" or, as used later, "justified." (30) Set was taken into custody, dragged before Osiris, and thrown to the ground where Osiris sat upon him as a sign of the triumph of good over evil. Set was banished to the Red Land, the foreign countries outside Egypt's borders, where he became identified with the evil gods and things of foreigners. Horus was awarded jurisdiction over the Black Land of Egypt itself.(31)

Having demonstrated that he was "true of word" Osiris now returned to his divine origins and ascended into heaven. Here he became the god of the dead presiding over the realm of the deceased which, over time, came to resemble an agricultural paradise to which all might aspire. Osiris lived with the gods and came to be the Great Judge, he who weighed the truthfulness of the hearts of the deceased to determine if the ethical quality of their lives merited eternal salvation. By the Sixth Dynasty Osiris was accepted throughout Egypt as the god who became man, who suffered, died, and was risen, and who lived forever with the gods were he sat in judgement of all men.

By the Pyramid Age the Osiris myth had become the central feature of Egyptian religion and Osiris himself a deity second only to Re. The incorporation of the Osiris myth into the state religion was the beginning of a process that eventually produced a complete theology of resurrection and eternal life for all men. By the Pyramid Age the Osiris myth contained all the basic elements of a new theological doctrine. Death, resurrection, judgement, and eternal life were all present if only in a form awaiting further theological definition. At this stage of its development the elements of the myth still applied only to the king. Since Osiris was perceived to have been a king as well, it was logical that his fate should be shared by other pharaohs. Egyptian theologians developed the Osiris myth more fully over a thousand years into an integrated theological doctrine connecting its elements by detailed theological reasoning. An important consequence of this was to extend the privileges of Osiris beyond the kings to include all humans. And so it came to be that Everyman could hope for justice and eternal life beyond the grave.

The process of theological refinement was not unlike that which occurred within Christianity. Although the mystical doctrines of Christianity were present in basic form from the very beginning, their articulation as a complete theological system took more than a thousand years to accomplish. The stimulus for the theological development of Christianity and the Osiris myth was identical, that is the need of theologians of both faiths to make sense of the mysteries and explain them to the faithful. Only a few years after the death of Jesus we find Saint Paul being queried by the Corinthians to explain the promise of resurrection. They inquire of Paul, "How are the dead to be raised up, and with what body do they come?" (32) In the development of their respective theologies of resurrection and eternal life Christianity and Egyptian religion were compelled first to develop a theory of the human personality whose terms and premises could be used to explain the religious claims of their respective faiths. The Christians took their view of man largely from Greek philosophy. Egyptian theologians, writing two thousand years before the rise of Classical Greece, developed a completely original idea of personhood that, as far as we know, was the first attempt at a written description of human nature in history.

Egyptian thinking on the human person was sophisticated and abstract and at least as complex as the later attempts by Greek philosophers that provided Christianity with many of the concepts to explain its theology. Although reflecting ideas that were first formulated during the Pyramid Age, a complete rendering of Egyptian notions concerning the human personality, resurrection, and eternal life was first expounded in the historically more recent *Book of the Dead*. It is important to recall that this "book" was a collection of prayers, spells, and instructions written on scrolls interred with the deceased to aid in the process of resurrection, surviving the judgement of Osiris, and gaining entry to the afterlife. The Egyptian emphasis on resurrection and eternal life is clearly evident in the title of the book. Its title is not properly the *Book of the Dead*, a title introduced by the Muslims after their conquest of Egypt in the seventh century and carried into the common vocabulary by later archeological use. The proper Egyptian title is the *Book of Coming Into Life*, and it was intended as a sacred handbook on how to attain resurrection and eternal life. (33) The Egyptians, like the Christians after them, were at great pains to explain "how the dead are to be raised up," and succeeded in developing an idea of the human person that made resurrection and eternal life seem possible.

The Egyptians conceived of a human nature comprised of eight distinct elements, each of which in some way shaped the physical and spiritual potentialities of a complete person. These elements were: (1) a physical body, (2) a spiritual body, (3) a heart, (4) a soul, (5) a shadow, (6) an intangible casing or spirit, (7) a form, and (8) a name. (34) Each provided a person with some defining element of individual life, such that one or more elements might be altered while another or others persisted unchanged. The human being's most basic form of existence and the one which is felt most continually on earth was the physical body or *khat*. The word itself was connected with something that would decay and was transitory. The physical body established a important *theological* connection between

man and god, for man was akin to Osiris in that both possessed a physical existence. No other Egyptian god ever became man, inhabited a physical body,
endured a human existence, and suffered death. The fact that only Osiris and
humans both possessed a physical body was what made it possible for humans to
believe that Osiris would be a merciful judge. Only Osiris in his human incarnation truly knew the temptations and sufferings that human beings must endure in
this life. Christian thinking on the subject of Jesus' human nature is strikingly
similar. A divine Jesus became truly human and suffered the same way any
human would suffer a crucifixion. It was through this human suffering that Jesus
made it possible for humans to attain eternal life.

Nowhere in Egyptian thinking, however, was there the promise that man's
corruptible body would rise from the earth and join the soul in eternal life. As we
have seen the idea persisted that the corruptible body had to be preserved as a
requirement of eternal life, although the understanding of the means by which
preservation might be achieved changed radically over the centuries. In the Pyramid Age the bodies of the pharaohs were sustained by constant rituals performed
within their mortuary temples while their embalmed bodies rested securely
within sealed tombs. By the end of the Feudal Age these practices had been
largely abandoned and replaced by embalming, symbolic rituals, periodic offerings, and burying magical amulets, prayers, and inscriptions as ways to preserve
the body in the tomb. Every Egyptian worried about how his body might fare
after he had passed on to the afterlife, for the ancient belief persisted that the eternal soul might cease to exist if the earthly body from which it had sprung was
destroyed.

Once embalmed and entombed, the natural body was transformed into a spiritual body or *sahu*. The transformation was accomplished by means of ritual and
prayers, most particularly the ceremony of "the opening of the mouth" whose ritual revivified the body in its new state. This transformation is described in the
Book of The Dead by such phrases as, "I germinate like the plants." "My flesh germinateth." "I exist, I exist, I live, I live, I germinate, I germinate," and "thy soul
liveth, thy body germinateth by the command of Re." (35) The *sahu* was often
portrayed as a mummy lying on a bier like the *khat*, but the two entities were
quite different. The *sahu* was a body that had been transformed by acquiring a
degree of knowledge, power, and glory which the *khat* or physical body did not
possess. The *sahu* is a "glorified" body which had become lasting and incorruptible even as the physical body itself would decay. In its glorified state the *sahu* had
the power to associate with the soul and converse with it. In this form the *sahu*
may even ascend into heaven and dwell with the *sahu* of the gods and the righ-

teous previously departed. (36) The idea of a glorified body found its way into later Christian thinking with the notion that the bodies of the deceased would one day be raised from the dead and rejoined with their souls to live eternally in heaven. The raised bodies would be perfected or glorified and live in this state forever.

A third essential element of the human personality was the *ab*, literally the heart of a man. The heart was very important to a person's character and to one's chances for being judged a worthy soul, for the *ab* was the seat of a person's power of life and the fountain of good and evil thoughts. (37) The heart was the seat of the intellect. A good heart was incapable of not telling the truth, and the Egyptian deceased often had amulets buried with them to prevent the heart from betraying them during the last judgement when the deceased were required to swear that they had not performed evil acts. It was the heart as the seat of truth that was weighed against a single feather to determine its truthfulness in the final judgement by Osiris. If the heart was true the deceased was pronounced *maet kheru* or "true of heart" and the judgement rendered favorably. The deceased was now said to be "justified." If the judgement was negative, the heart of the deceased was thrown to the "Devourer of Hearts," a terrible beast with the head of a crocodile, the body of a lion, and the hind quarters of a hippopotamus that waited beside the scales of judgement to be fed. The monster ate the wanting heart on the spot, whereupon the deceased suffered the most horrible of Egyptian fates, "the Second Dying," in which he ceased to exist forever. Egyptian theologians never conceived of a hell of eternal suffering. Evil persons simply ceased to exist. (38)

It is puzzling that a people so accustomed to embalming corpses that required the removal of internal organs failed to develop a more accurate biology of the human body. Egyptian physicians developed sophisticated surgical techniques for treating skull fractures including the ability to lift the crushed skull from the dura of the brain. (39) And yet they attributed no personality function to the brain, locating the intellect in the heart instead. During embalming the brain case was entered through the nose by a long handled spoon-shaped instrument used to scoop out the organ's soft matter. Egyptian physicians were aware of pulse and fever, but not of circulation of the blood. They believed that veins carried air and terminated not at the heart but at the anus. (40)

In addition to a human's natural and spiritual body a person possessed an abstract personality or individuality endowed with all his physical, moral, and psychological characteristics. When a person was conceived, Egyptian theologians believed that the god Khnum fashioned the child upon a potter's wheel. At the same time Khnum fashioned an exact double or image of the child called the *ka*. Identical to the person in every way, the *ka* nonetheless had an independent existence. The *ka* could move about freely and unite or separate itself from the body or even travel to and reside in heaven among the gods. The hieroglyph for *ka* is a pair of upraised arms and its meaning translates as image, genius, double, character, and even mental attributes. The *ka* could dwell anyplace, and it was common to place a statue of the deceased within the tomb to become the dwelling place of the *ka*. Just as the Egyptians believed that a god "dwelled" incarnate within a statue of himself so, too, might the *ka* of a man dwell within the statue of a person. In this regard the *ka* seems identical to the *sekhem* or image that dwelled within a statue.

From the very earliest time Egyptian tombs were equipped with a small chapel (the *ka* chapel) where the *ka* was visited and received offerings. It was common to fashion a false door on the wall of the chapel with a relief of the deceased walking through it toward the viewer. Here the *ka* priests or family visitors provided sustenance to the *ka*. The *ka* could consume food and in the Pyramid Age food and drink were placed daily before the *ka* for it to eat. The *ka* did not consume the food of course, but was said to consume the essence or substance of the food. The material remains were then eaten or sold by the priests. Here we find the first example of the basic philosophical distinction between substance and accident that was so important to later Greek philosophy and which appeared in the Christian theology of the Eucharist wherein the substance of the god's body and blood was said to be present and consumed by worshippers while the material accidents of bread and wine remained unchanged. The Egyptian idea that the spiritual body depended upon a constant supply of sepulchral offerings took hold during the early Pyramid Age. As the idea of resurrection spread to the common man by the Feudal Age it was clear that such arrangements were neither practical nor possible, so that from this time the *ka* was said to sustain itself even more abstractly by consuming the essence of the portrayals of food and drink painted and carved on the tomb walls. (41)

The part of man that was believed to be eternal and to enjoy an eternal glorified existence in heaven was the *ba*, a word that literally translates as "sublime" or "noble" but whose theological meaning can be accurately rendered as "soul." Although it dwelled in the *ka* and was, like the heart, the principle of animated life, the *ba* possessed both form and substance. In form it was depicted as a small human-headed hawk shown hovering over the body or exiting from the mouth of the deceased. Portrayals depicting the soul leaving the body in the same manner can be found in early Christian art. The substance of the *ba* is less easily defined and is most commonly said to be "refined" or "ethereal," (42) terms also used by the Greeks to describe the "shades" of people cast into Hades, and by Greek philosophers of the atomist tradition to describe the soul or mind. The *ba* possessed an independent existence but was said to "become a soul" only once the body of the deceased had been revivified by prayer and ritual. (43) Once free, the *ba* could move about wherever it wished and could take upon itself any shape. It could move freely between heaven and the *ka* in the tomb, and it could revisit the body and reanimate and converse with it. (44)

Along with the *ka* the *ba* partook of funerary offerings, and in the Pyramid Age it was thought that the *ba*'s continued existence depended upon its being sustained by food and drink. Later this belief was modified so that, like the *ka*, the *ba* could be sustained by the pictorial representations of sustenance carved on the tomb walls. Once given relief from the material realm by the death and reanimation of the corpse, the permanent dwelling place of the *ba* was in heaven where it would "mingle with the gods and become them." (45) Once more we encounter the idea that the soul "mingles" with the gods in a way strikingly similar to the Christian idea that the souls of the departed join with god and the angels. The *ba* in heaven was a glorified soul that sat among the gods and ate what they ate, drank what they drank so that "he thirsts not, he hungers not, nor is he sad." The deceased in heaven wears the apparel of the gods, white linen and sandals, and "he goeth to the great lake in the midst of the Field of Peace whereon the great gods sit." He eats of the "bread of eternity" and drinks the "beer of everlastingness" and he is washed clean. (46)

Egyptian theologians appear to have been the first people to conceive of the idea of a soul as an animating principle of human material existence that was, in itself, immaterial in substance and immortal in nature so that its existence persisted beyond the death of the material body. The idea of a soul was among the earliest theological concepts invented by the Egyptians, appearing for the first time in written form during the Pyramid Age but having existed for at least a millennium before that in Egyptian religious thinking as contained in the Osiris myth. The idea of an immortal soul did not, however, characterize the theological thinking of any other major near eastern or western culture of the ancient world. None of these cultures—Sumerian, Babylonian, Canaanite, Israelite, Persian, Iranian, Greek or Roman—developed the idea on their own, and none except the Greek and Roman cultures adopted it after contact with the Egyptians. Greek thinking about the soul during the Classical Age was derived from the philosophical system of Plato that drew heavily upon the ancient idea that the material world was but a pale reflection of the divine world perceived by men as through a glass darkly.(47) It was not until the Christian era that the concept of an immortal soul was thoroughly incorporated into another theological system.

Another element of the human personality was the *khaibit* or shadow, and may be compared to the *umbra* or shade of the Romans and Greeks. Although the *khaibit* can be identified in the earliest Pyramid Texts, its specific role in personhood is not easily established. (48) As with other elements, the *khaibit* had an independent existence and was free to move about and could visit the tomb at will and partake of the funerary offerings. Curiously, both men and gods possessed a *khaibit*, and it was quite clear that it was associated with the soul and was always near it. Our understanding of Egyptian theology remains incomplete and the function of the *khaibit* remains mysterious. What is clear, however, is that Egyptian thinking about it and the other parts of the human personality was sufficiently abstract as to be properly called philosophical, and that Egyptian theologians must have spent long hours contemplating and discussing just what it was that made a human being human. It is true as well that our understanding of their thinking on such abstract subjects is far less complete and precise than theirs was at the time. While other cultures had their theologies, the depth, breadth, complexity, and level of abstraction of Egyptian religious thinking make it difficult to escape the impression that Egyptian theologians gave the world the first theology worthy of the name.

The *khu* of a person was the shining or translucent intangible casing of the body. The word itself can be translated as intelligence, shining one, or glorious, and, perhaps, aura, but it may be safely rendered as spirit as well. The Pyramid Texts tell that the *khu's* of the gods lived with them in heaven and the *khu* of the deceased made its way to heaven as soon as the prayers over the body rendered it animate again enabling the *khu* to depart. The *khu* is a mysterious entity and it is best to admit that our knowledge of Egyptian theology is insufficient to truly understand its nature or function. The same may be said of another part of the human personality, that is the *sekhem*. As Budge notes, the word may be rendered as power or form, "but it is very difficult to find any expression that will represent the Egyptian conception of the *sekhem*," (49) except that it is always mentioned in connection with the soul.

We are unable to determine which of these elements of human nature possessed a priority of existence or importance in achieving eternal life. The important point is that the Egyptians believed that several elements had to be present for a complete human being to exist, and when any necessary element was absent something less than a person was left. It was an old Babylonian idea later adopted by the Jews and Greeks that upon a person's death his defining substance departed leaving behind a partial or monstrous quasi-human who might continue to exist is some vague way. The Greek idea of a person's "shade" as being humanly incomplete parallels the type of deformed humans found in the Mesopotamian conception of the *etimmu* or ghost and those who dwelt in the Hebrew *Sheol.* (50) There seems to be no Egyptian equivalent of this idea. With no idea of a tormenting hell, Egyptian theologians could safely ignore what happened to people when they went to such terrible places.

The Egyptian emphasis on life after death led of necessity to the question of how this might be achieved. Egyptian theology preserved a role and function for each element of human personhood in the hereafter just as the various elements were required for a truly human life on earth. Even the body did not merely decay in either a physical or spiritual sense, but was transformed into something else. The soul may be the primary entity that is eternal, but it is accompanied, supported, and facilitated by other elements in the human person in the process of becoming and remaining immortal. Whatever else Egyptian theological contemplation on the subject of the soul and its eternal life it was remarkably comprehensive.

The Feudal Age saw a theology of resurrection and eternal life emerge from its beginning in the articulation of the ideals of the Osiris myth through to the application of the concepts of the Egyptian psychology of human personhood. This theological formulation was accompanied by an expansion of the promise of Osiris and the new faith to include the common man. Once restricted to Egyptian kings, the hope of victory over death was now extended to all Egyptians. Democratization was already evident in the 11th Dynasty where important ritual changes signalled the universalization of the Osiris theology. For the first time it became the regular custom to attach the word "justified" to the name of every deceased suggesting that the deceased had successfully passed the last judgement and achieved immortality. For the first time the name Osiris was formally inserted as a title before the name of the deceased in all inscriptions signifying that the deceased had "become one with god." The clearest indication that the former privileges of kings had been extended to the common man was the addition of divine symbols upon the coffin lids of ordinary people. Since the deceased was identified with the god Osiris, the coffins of the deceased bearing the visage of the corpse were now commonly ordained with the false beard and ureaus of the pharaoh, both ancient symbols of divinity. (51)

The old mortuary rituals where *ka* priests provided food and prayer offerings for the dead had fallen into disuse replaced first by inscriptions of ritual prayer and food on the coffins of the deceased (the Coffin Texts) and, by the end of the

Feudal Age, by the common practice of interring sacred prayer scrolls (the *Book of the Dead*) and magical amulets with the deceased. One of the most complete scrolls, the Ani Papyrus, provided archaeologists with a vivid and comprehensive portrayal of the key elements of the new Osiris theology. The Ani Papyrus dates from the New Kingdom when these scrolls were in wide use, but its contents are certainly much older, testifying to the millennium-long efforts of Egyptian theologians to flesh out the ideals of the Osiris myth with a conceptual explanation of how resurrection, judgement, and eternal life were to be achieved. (52) How ancient that effort might have been is suggested by the fact that some parts of the Ani Papyrus refer to events and subjects that date to before the First Dynasty when the Osiris myth was already evident if only in its application to Egyptian kings. By the beginning of the New Kingdom the Osiris theology was fully developed and widely accepted so that all the faithful knew "how the dead are raised up and with what body they come."

An Egyptian of Ani's time reading the *Book of the Dead* would have learned that his soul would undergo three separate judgements by the gods as an assessment of his moral worth to merit eternal life. (53) It is likely that these different versions of judgement were originally independent, but over the centuries came to be assembled into a single portrayal of the final judgement. (54) The first judgement is explained in the *Chapter of Entering the Hall of Truth*. The text explains what the soul can expect when "purged from all evil that he has done, and he beholds the face of the god." The deceased's soul begins by greeting the Great God and preparing to assert the soul's freedom from sin. Here we encounter what early archaeologists mistakenly called the First Confession. It must be clearly understood that the term "confession" is inappropriate, for the soul is not confessing at all. Neither Egyptian ethics nor theology had yet developed the concept of personal sin that would come later. What the deceased is doing is testifying to his own character by swearing that he lived a proper ethical life. The list of moral precepts to which the soul must swear is quite impressive, and testifies unambiguously to the depth and breadth of the Egyptian concern with individual and social ethics. By Egyptian standards the *Decalogue of Moses* is sparse indeed. The affirmation of the soul in the first of the three judgments is as follows.

> *"Behold, I came to thee, I bring to thee righteousness and I expel for thee sin. I have*
>
> *committed no sin against the people....I have not done evil in the place of truth. I knew*

no wrong. I did no evil thing….I did not do that which the god abominates. I did not

report evil of a servant to his master. I allowed no one to hunger. I caused no one to

weep. I did not murder. I did not command to murder. I caused no man misery. I did not diminish food in the temples. I did not decrease the offerings of the gods. I did

not take away the food-offerings of the dead. I did not commit adultery. I did not commit self-pollution in the pure precinct of my city-god. I did not diminish the grain

measure. I did not diminish the span. I did not diminish the land measure. I did not

load the weight of the balances. I did not deflect the index of the scales. I did not take milk from the mouth of the child. I did not drive away the cattle from their pasturage. I did not snare the fowl of the gods. I did not catch the fish in their pools. I did not hold back the water in its time. I did not dam the running water. I did not quench the fire in its time. I did not withhold the herds of the temple endowments. I did not interfere with the god in his payments." (55)

While there are a few items that refer to personal moral behavior and others dealing with proper ritual behavior, it is noteworthy that most of the precepts deal with proper *social* behavior. Thus one does not cheat one's neighbor by altering the scales or measures or take more than one's fair share of water during dry times. The Egyptians believed that ethics properly understood was at base a public social contract and was not to be confused with personal character or even law which they recognized to be no guarantee of proper ethical behavior. In the First Judgement of the soul the importance of this view of ethics as social action and restraint is clearly reflected in the preponderance of precepts that exceed personal or ritual requirements.

The soul now passed into the presence of Osiris the Great Judge who sat at the end of a grand hall accompanied by 42 gods who assisted him in the judgement of the dead. Each god originally represented one of the 42 *nomes* or districts of ancient Egypt. They are terrifying demons possessed of grotesque names like

"Shadow Eater that Came out of the Cave" or "Blood-Eater that Came out of the Place of Execution." The soul calls out to each god in turn calling each by name and making a declaration of innocence of some particular misdeed. In this Second Confession which, once again, is not really a confession but an affirmation of innocence, the soul once more swears to its high ethical character.

In the Second Confession there appears to be a shift away from social ethics to considerations of personal character, and only minor mentions of ritual obligations are present. The soul testified to its personal character by such affirmations as "I did not speak lies, I did not make falsehood in the place of truth, I was not deaf to truthful words, I was not avaricious, my heart coveted not, my heart was not hasty, I did not multiply words in speaking, my voice was not overly loud, my mouth did not wag, I did not revile, and I was not an eavesdropper." Along the same lines the soul testified to its proper sexual conduct by affirming "I did not commit adultery with a woman, and I did not commit self-pollution." The Egyptian concern for social ethics is evident in the declarations of the soul that "I did not slay men, I did not rob, I did not steal, I did not rob one crying for his possessions, my fortune was not great but by my own property, I did not take away food, I did not stir up fear, I did not stir up strife and I did not diminish the grain measure." As regards ritual obligations, the soul swears that "I did not revile the king, I did not blaspheme the god, I did not slay the divine bull, I did not steal the temple endowment, I did not diminish the food in the temple, and I did not do an abomination of the gods." With these statements the soul affirms that it is worthy of being accepted into eternal life and says, "Behold, I come to you without sin, without evil, without wrong….I live on righteousness, I feed on the righteousness of my heart. I have done that which men say, and that wherewith the gods are content." (56)

The soul then moved closer to the end of the great hall where Osiris sat enthroned with Isis and Nephthys standing behind him. Along one side of the hall are arranged the nine gods of the Heliopolitan Ennead, headed by the Sun-god, an arrangement which indicates the solar origins of the judgement of the deceased but in which Osiris, not Re, has assumed the place of central importance. (57) At Osiris' feet are the scales of justice, "the balances of Re wherewith he weighs truth." The jackal-god Anubis operates the scales while Toth, the scribe of the gods, presides over the weighing of the heart with pen and writing palette in hand to record the verdict. Behind Toth crouches the monstrous Devourer of Hearts. In the Ani Papyrus Renenet and Meskhenet, the two goddesses of birth, stand contemplating the fate of the soul over which they had presided when the soul first came into the world. Standing at the entrance of the hall is the goddess "Truth, Daughter of Re," who ushers the newly arrived soul, Ani, into the hall.

Ani enters the hall with head bowed. At once Anubis calls for his heart represented by the hieroglyph of a small vase which is placed upon the scale. A single white feather, the hieroglyph for truth, is placed upon the opposing balance. Slowly the scale moves from side to side seeking its center. It is at this dramatic moment that the soul pleads with his own heart not to betray him. "Oh my heart that came from my mother! Oh my heart belonging to my own being! Rise not up against me as a witness....Be not hostile to me before the master of the balances....Let not my name be of evil odor with the court, speak no lie against me in the presence of the god." (58) With this the scale stops showing Ani's heart and the feather of truth to be in balance. Perhaps it was this Egyptian portrayal of the final judgement with scales that produced the image found in the Old Testament that one had been weighed in the balance and been found not wanting. It is not unreasonable to surmise that the image of the judgement of Osiris made its way into Israelite culture along with much of Egyptian wisdom literature.

The soul having been weighed and found true, Toth announces the verdict to the council. "Hear ye this word in truth. I have judged the heart of Osiris Ani. His soul stands as a witness concerning him, his character is just by the great balances. No sin of his has been found." Here we see the joining of the deceased's name, Ani, with that of the god, Osiris, indicating that the soul and the god have in some mystical sense become one. All justified souls, then, become gods or at least god-like. The Nine Gods of the Ennead respond to Toth's verdict with joy. "How good it is, this which comes forth from thy just mouth. Osiris Ani, the justified, witnesses. There is no sin of his, there is no evil of his with us....Let there be given to him the bread that cometh forth before Osiris, the domain that abideth in the field of offerings, like the Flowers of Horus." Ani is now led before Osiris by Horus, the son of Osiris and Isis, who presents him to the Great God. "I come to thee, Osiris; I bring to thee Osiris Ani. His righteous heart comes forth from the balances and he has no sin in the sight of any god or goddess. Toth has judged him in writing; the Nine Gods have spoken concerning him a very just testimony. Let there be given to him the bread and beer that come forth before Osiris-Wennofer like the Followers of Horus." Holding the hand of Horus Ani addresses Osiris. "Lo, I am before thee, Lord of The West. There is no sin in my body....Let me be like the favorites who are in thy following." (59) Ani kneels before the Great God and presents a table of offerings and is received into the kingdom of Osiris to live forever.

Once underway the inclusion of the common man in the hope of resurrection and eternal life revolutionized the practice of Egyptian religion. Thousands of shrines and temples were constructed to Osiris and the sacred temple to Osiris at Abydos, the mystical site of Osiris' burial, resurrection, and ascension was expanded to accommodate thousands of pilgrims who visited the site to obtain special blessings. The wealthy and powerful sought to be buried at Abydos, and the less well-off had the mummies of the deceased sent there to be blessed before interment elsewhere. The annual "passion play" portraying the death and resurrection of Osiris drew thousands of spectators. Throughout the land priests, scribes, undertakers, and craftsmen became rich through the sale of burial scrolls and amulets that facilitated a proper judgement and resurrection that were buried with the deceased. Within a few years the worship of Osiris had become the primary religion of the common man. Until the New Kingdom the official religion of the state had been the worship of the solar Re. During the imperial period Re was joined with Ptah and Amun to form a new trinity at the center of state worship. But outside the confines of official ritual the Egyptians worshipped the god that promised them eternal life and justice. Over the next fifteen hundred years, until displaced by Christianity, the worship of Osiris, Isis, and Horus gradually overwhelmed all other Egyptian cults. By the third century B.C.E., Osiris had superseded even Re himself.

It is difficult for people in the modern age to appreciate the attraction of Osiris for the ordinary Egyptian. For most people in modern times religion represents but one element of their lives. In ancient Egypt religion was central to a person's life as well as the life of the state which remained a theocracy of sorts until the end. To be included in the hope of resurrection and eternal life must have excited the common man in ways modern men can only imagine. Egyptians believed without question for millennia that their kings lived beyond the grave. Now the common man might do so too. Centuries later Christians would greet the same news of eternal life with the same great hope and call it "gospel," or good news. And good news it was for Egyptian and Christian alike. Life in the ancient world was often harsh and unjust, and until Osiris there was no escape or hope of justice. With Osiris came both, and this hope survived to become a central tenet of the major religion of Western civilization. The prospect of a judgement beyond the grave had a profound effect on Egyptian ethics in that Osiris offered yet another incentive for man to behave properly toward his neighbor. It was no accident that the later Egyptian Wisdom Literature made reference to the need for humans to act ethically lest they be "weighed in the balance and found wanting."

The formalization and democratization of the Osiran theology marked the last great theological innovation of Egyptian thinkers and it would become, albeit more than a thousand years later, Egypt's greatest intellectual contribution to the culture of the West. By the middle of the New Kingdom (1552-1069 B.C.E.) the worship of Osiris had assumed paramount importance in the religious life of most Egyptians. The official state religion still worshiped the Ptah-Re-Amun trinity with Amun assuming the dominant position at the insistence of the Theban warrior pharaohs who forged the Egyptian empire and wished a national place for their local god. The national religious establishment created by Thutmose III now threatened the secular authority of the state itself, and by the end of the rule of the Rameside pharaohs (1069 B.C.E.), the Egyptian king had yielded the scepter to the head of what had become a state church.

The religious establishment led by the high priest of Amun imposed a sacerdotal state upon Lower Egypt while the pharaoh governed Upper Egypt from the Delta capital of Tanis. The sacerdotal state focused upon magic and ritual and in outward form took on the trappings of religious dignity and splendor in all aspects of its existence. It was during this time that some of the most impressive religious architecture in Egyptian history was constructed. Priestly garments and temple interiors were lavish and ritual observance dominated the day. In many ways it was not unlike the period of cathedral building in Europe prior to the Renaissance when priestly rule and public devotion coalesced in great public acts of faith expressed in material ways.

The sacerdotal state was the beginning of the end of Egyptian religion which became overly formalized, ritualistic, and intellectually ossified. With the exception of the common faith of Osiris which continued to spread and remain a meaningful religious commitment for those who adhered to it, Egyptian religion lost its vitality and its inner power of development. The more its priests clung to their rituals and prerogatives, the less able was the religion to make itself relevant to the everyday life of the ordinary Egyptian. The evidence of this gap was already present in the sacerdotal period when it became common to write the name of Osiris by means of the hieroglyph of the sun-disk instead of the usual image of the eye of Horus. (60) The official importance of Amun in the state religion and the increasing unofficial importance of Osiris among the populace logically led to a decline in the importance of Re in religious observance. Osiris gradually absorbed Re until he became "the ruler who occupied the seat of Re," that is, Osiris had become the successor of Re. By the Ptolemaic period in the 3rd century B.C.E. the worship of Re had all but disappeared, replaced by the new trinity of Orisis, Isis, and Horus. (61)

The decline in religious vitality paralleled a decline in other areas of Egyptian national life. It was during the sacerdotal period that Nubia was lost to Egypt as a line of powerful kings emerged to direct its own national destiny. Through the 22nd Dynasty (945-715 B.C.E.), Egypt suffered a succession of eight Libyan mercenary kings who transformed Egypt into a military state and eventually destroyed the sacerdotal regime at Thebes by appointing their sons as chief priests of the temple of Amun. While the Libyans paid lip-service to the worship of Amun, their true loyalties lay with the worship of Bastet, the goddess of cats. When the Libyan dynasty was finally overthrown by the 25th Dynasty (747-525 B.C.E.) of Ethiopian kings, the worship of Amun at Thebes was on its last legs. Before gaining its independence Nubia had been subjected to a millennium of Egyptian rule so that the Ethiopians had become more Egyptian than the Egyptians! The Ethiopian kings considered themselves the true heirs to the Egyptian religious tradition and the worship of Amun. When the Ethiopian king Piankhy conquered Egypt around 730 B.C.E., he took great care to spare the temples and shrines. He unified the country and took pains to attend the old religious services and present offerings to the old gods. Piankhy considered himself an orthodox Egyptian and treated the Egyptian dynasts with scorn. (62)

The Ethiopians set about reestablishing the old Egypt first by reestablishing Egyptian political unity and then by developing religion, architecture, and art to rekindle Egypt's great past. They chose the Old Kingdom as the model of how things ought to be, and for more than a century they supported programs of rebuilding and reanimating the character and ritual of ancient life. (63) In 663 B.C.E. Ethiopia stumbled into a war with Assurbanipal of Assyria whose armies captured Thebes and laid waste the Theban temples. The Ethiopians retreated to their homeland and never returned to Egypt. With their departure the great Amun of Thebes lost his place in the Egyptian state religion and reverted to his previous stature as a local god never to rise again. Within a decade a new native Egyptian dynasty, the 26th (660-525 B.C.E.), arose under Psammetichus I with its capital at Sais in the Delta. The archaizing tendency that had begun under the Ethiopians was continued with great success under the 26th Dynasty, and many of the forms and practices of the Old Kingdom were rekindled.

During this time the Osiris faith retained its vitality and attractiveness to the common man unhindered by state religious policies. Underneath it all, however, Egypt was weak and the kings of the 26th Dynasty were forced to rely upon Greek mercenaries to garrison their frontier fortresses. In 525 B.C.E., the armies of the Persian king Cambyses II reached Egypt's borders. After sporadic resistance, Egypt was overwhelmed. But apart from stationing their own troops in

Egypt and levying an imperial tax, the Persians made no attempt to change the institutions of the country and did not interfere in Egyptian religious life. The influence and popularity of Osiris worship continued as did the decline of both Re and Amun. By the time Alexander the Great conquered Egypt in 332 B.C.E., the worship of Re and Amun was almost non-existent while Osiris, Isis, and Horus, were firmly established as the only trinitarian god.

Alexander's conquest brought Egypt into its first sustained contact with the West and served as the mechanism for the transmission of Egyptian theological ideas into the theologies of the West. Both Greek and Roman religious traditions were strongly influenced by the theological principles associated with the worship of Osiris whose cult was now more widespread and influential than it had ever been in its history. The Osiran theological principles that were passed to the West were precisely those noted at the start of this chapter: (1) the belief in a single god expressed in trinitarian form; (2) a cosmology in which all things have a place that can be comprehended by humans; (3) the belief in an immortal soul; (4) the belief in the resurrection of the dead; (5) the belief in a final judgement of the quality of a man's ethical life; (6) an affirmative judgement as a requirement for achieving eternal life beyond death. *It is important to understand that none of these ideas had yet made their appearance in any other theology of the West or the Near East.* While the theology of the Israelites had by this time incorporated some Egyptian thinking, Judaism then (and now) never incorporated any of the fundamental theological principles of the Osiris theology. Whenever we discover any Osiran theological principles reflected in the theologies of the West, there is no other logical or historical source for them but Egypt.

NOTES

1. E.A. Wallis Budge, *Egyptian Ideas of the Afterlife* (New York: Dover Publications, 1995), 14.

2. A.H. Gardiner, "Notes on the Ethics of the Egyptians," *Ancient Egypt*, vol. 2 (1914), 55-56.

3. Joseph Scott and Lenore Scott, *Egyptian Hieroglyphics For Everyone: An Introduction to the Writings of Ancient Egypt* (New York: Barnes and Noble, 1993), 23.

4. E.A. Wallis Budge, *The Egyptian Book of The Dead* (New York: Dover Publications, 1967), xlviii.

5. Christine Hobson, *The World of the Pharaohs* (London: Thames and Hudson, 1987), 168.

6. James H. Breasted, *The Dawn of Conscience* (New York: Charles Scribner, 1947), 106.

7. Ibid., 111.

8. Budge, *The Egyptian Book of the Dead*, xlvii.

9. Breasted, 45.

10. Ibid., 95.

11. E.A. Wallis Budge, *Osiris and the Egyptian Resurrection* vol. 1 (New York: Dover Publications, 1973), 66.

12. Ibid., 175.

13. Ibid., 167.

14. Breasted, 45.

15. Budge, *Osiris and the Egyptian Resurrection*, 200-204.

16. Ibid., 208.

17. Hobson, 52.

18. Ibid., 53.

19. Ibid.

20. James H. Breasted, *The Development of Religion and Thought In Ancient Egypt* (New York: Harper and Brothers, 1959), 38-39.

21. Budge, *Egyptian Ideas of the Afterlife*, 41; see also Breasted, *The Dawn of Conscience*, 97.

22. Budge, *Osiris and the Egyptian Resurrection*, 79.

23. Hobson, 56.

24. Ibid., 144.

25. Breasted, *The Dawn of Conscience*, 27.

26. Ibid., 101.

27. James Breasted records his own experience with scorpions in Egypt along similar lines. Breasted notes that he came upon a peasant in the Delta whose dog had been stung by a scorpion and was dying. Another farmer told the man of an ancient cure for scorpion bites. The dog was wrapped in linen and placed in a shallow tub of warm water as his body was stroked until the animal fell asleep. After some hours in a deep slumber the dog awoke and recovered. Breasted notes that this same treatment is the one that was administered to Horus in the story of the attempt by the scorpion god on the child's life.

28. Breasted, *The Dawn of Conscience*, 31.

29. Budge, *Osiris and the Egyptian Resurrection*, 96.

30. Ibid., 309.

31. Jaroslav Cerny, *Ancient Egyptian Religion* (Westport, CT: Greenwood Press, 1979), 125.

32. *1 Corinthians*, 15:35

33. Scott and Scott, 83. The title can also be translated as the Book of Coming into the Day, or the Dawn.

34. Budge, *The Egyptian Book of the Dead*, lxix.

35. Ibid., lix

36. Ibid., lx.

37. Ibid. lxi.

38. Budge, *Osiris and the Egyptian Resurrection*, 328.

39. Richard A. Gabriel and Karen S. Metz, *A History of Military Medicine*, vol. 1 (Westport, CT: Greenwood Press, 1992), 77.

40. Ibid., 80.

41. Budge, *The Egyptian Book of the Dead*, lxiii.

42. Ibid., lxiv.

43. Breasted, *The Dawn of Conscience*, 47-48.

44. Budge, *The Egyptian Book of the Dead*, lxiv.

45. Ibid.

46. Ibid., lxxvi.

47. Karen Armstrong, *A History of God* (New York: Ballantine Books, 1993), 35.

48. Budge, *The Egyptian Book of the Dead*, lxvi.

49. Ibid., lxvii.

50. S.G.F. Brandon, *Religion in Ancient History* (New York: Charles Scribner's Sons, 1969), 75; 113.

51. Rosalie David, *The Cult of the Sun: Myth and Magic in Ancient Egypt* (New York: Barnes and Noble, 1998), 133.

52. Budge, *The Egyptian Book of the Dead*, xii.

53. The description of the final judgement that follows is derived from several sources to compensate for differences in translation and emphasis. The sources most heavily relied upon are the works of Breasted and Budge, all already noted herein. Budge's work is most commonly regarded as the most original and seminal.

54. Breasted, *The Dawn of Conscience*, 255.

55. This is Breasted's translation of Budge, *Dawn of Conscience*, 255; see also in Budge, "Chapter of Entering into the Hall of Truth," *The Egyptian Book of the Dead*, cli.

56. Budge, ibid., 299.

57. Breasted, *The Dawn of Conscience*, 260.

58. Budge, *The Egyptian Book of the Dead*, 309.

59. Breasted, *The Dawn of Conscience*, 262.

60. Cerny, 137-138.

61. Ibid., 138.

62. Ibid., 131.

63. Ibid., 133.

3

Osiris and Christ:
The Historical Connection

In the spring of 334 B.C.E, Alexander the Great crossed the Hellespont in his war against the Persian Empire. In May he conquered the satraps of modern Turkey and Lebanon, and in that autumn he defeated Darius at the battle of Issus. With this victory the whole of the western Persian empire fell into Alexander's hands. Alexander turned south and marched down the Mediterranean coast breaking the resistance of the city-states of coastal Palestine until in the autumn of the following year, he crossed the Nile and entered Egypt. The Persian governor of Egypt, Amyntas, handed over his authority to the Macedonian king without resistance. (1) That same year the Oracle of Amun proclaimed Alexander the new Master of the Universe and three hundred years of Greek rule over Egypt began. Alexander was dead within a decade, precipitating a struggle for succession among his generals that fractured the empire into three realms. Egypt and the Mediterranean coastal states as far north as Ionia fell under the control of the Ptolemies who ruled Egypt for three hundred years until the last Ptolemaic queen, Cleopatra, lost the country to Roman ambitions in 30 B.C.E.

The period of Ptolemaic rule in Egypt from 322 to 30 B.C.E. is important because it was during this time that the worship of Osiris completely eclipsed the worship of Amun-Re, becoming the official state religion for the first time in Egyptian history. It was during this same period that personal piety and a recognition of sin emerged as major characteristics of the Osiran faith, completing the conception of a linkage between the individual and a personal god that had begun almost a millennium earlier. It was a time, too, when Osiris, always the god of the dead, replaced Re as a god of the living, the deity to whom people prayed for divine intervention in human affairs. Horus, the son of Osiris, came to be seen as a primary intermediary between Osiris and men in pleading their cases to his father. At the same time Isis became a central figure in the Osiris cult emerging as a powerful goddess to be worshipped in her own right. By the end of the Ptolemaic period the Egyptians had given the world the image of a holy family with Osiris as the father, Horus as the son, and Isis as the mother, all to be worshipped either individually—for they all were seen to promise eternal life—or together in the form of a new trinity.

Among the most amazing and important events of the Ptolemaic period was the establishment of the cult of the Egyptian Osiris trinity as the official religion of a state ruled by Macedonian Greeks with the result that *the cult of Isis spread throughout the Mediterranean world becoming the most popular religion of the age.* The cult of Isis, Osiris, and Horus was transmitted to Rome where, by the time of Christ, it had become the most popular religious faith of Romans, especially Roman soldiers. The period of Ptolemaic rule in Egypt succeeded in preserving and reinvigorating the four thousand year-old Egyptian religious tradition and passing it on to the West. W.E. Ritt has noted that during Christianity's formative years the religion of Isis was attracting converts from every corner of the Roman Empire, just as it had attracted the population of the Greek empire. Isis' priests were no mere passive practitioners of the obscure, but dedicated missionaries, like soldiers crusading in a hallowed service. (2) Mendicant priests and laymen travelled throughout the empire spreading the "good news" of salvation and resurrection. Long before St. Paul spread the good news to the Christians, the priests and lay followers of Isis had spread their gospel to the people of the Mediterranean basin.

Egypt under Greek rule retained its identity until the end of the Ptolemaic period. The problem faced by Ptolemy was how to govern Egypt with a small number of Greeks. Greek mercenaries had been living in Egypt for more than two hundred years before Alexander, and Greek traders and immigrants were not an uncommon sight. But Egypt was a country of between seven and nine million people (3), while the number of Greeks living there during the Ptolemaic period probably never exceeded 500,000. (4). At the time Ptolemy I (322-283 B.C.E.) assumed control of Egypt the number of Greeks was considerably less. Ptolemy faced the same problem that the Babylonians, Persians, and Alexander had faced in their respective imperial realms and solved it the same way, by leaving the existing politico-social system intact and imposing upon it a new ruling class. Ptolemy retained the old Pharaonic system where all land and resources were owned by the sovereign. Ptolemy ruled Egypt as his own property, a personal monopoly governed in his name by a horde of bureaucrats and an army of priests, both resting upon the broad base of the Egyptian peasantry. (5) For the vast majority of Egyptians life under the Greeks remained very much the same as it had always been, including the pattern of their religious practice.

The Egyptian bureaucracy and priesthood remained largely unchanged under Ptolemy I except that the estates of the priests were now perceived as belonging to the Greek king and not to pharaoh. The governmental infrastructure, including the legal system, was also retained. Ptolemy understood that he could not govern every part of a multi-cultural empire with the same set of laws. (6) Accordingly, Egyptian law continued to apply to Egyptians while Greek law applied to Greeks. Egyptians had their own judges, courts, and legal procedures that were very different from those that dealt with Greeks. While Greeks held key appointments to keep the system running smoothly, the Ptolemies were no less dependent than the pharaohs upon the old Egyptian bureaucrats and priests to keep the system operating. Ptolemy created a national council comprised of Egyptian priests, high ranking bureaucrats, and his own advisors to work out any problems of jurisdiction and authority.(7)

The power of the Egyptian priesthood was also reflected in its retention of the traditional power of asylum granted to the temples. Since time immemorial mistreated Egyptian workers had refused to work as a means of protesting unjust working conditions, the world's first labor strikes. When punishment was threatened the strikers sought asylum in the temples where they were beyond the reach of the civil authorities. At first Ptolemy curtailed this power of the Egyptian priests, but soon relented. Disputes between Greek overseers and Egyptian workers came to frequently involve priests whom the common man saw as their protectors, with the result that the Egyptian priesthood retained the respect it had possessed for generations in the eyes of the Egyptian citizenry.

Egypt thrived under the Ptolemies. Greek entrepreneurs stimulated trade with the outside world requiring Egyptian agriculture to produce surpluses for export. Although iron weapons had been used in Egypt for centuries, it was the Greeks who introduced iron agricultural implements to the Egyptian economy. (8) The Greeks also introduced a money economy on the Persian model, replacing the old in-kind payment system. Ptolemy himself took a direct interest in the export of papyrus which became the most commonly used writing material in the Mediterranean world. Egypt itself must have been among the best customers. The Library at Alexandria alone had 700,000 scrolls in its possession.(9)

The Ptolemies controlled the coastal city-states all along the Mediterranean littoral north to Ionia. These states became key trading ports with the result that the Ptolemies built a large navy that controlled the Mediterranean from Ionia and Phoenicia to the Aegean and as far west as Carthage and Sicily. These northern coastal ports were also the termini for the overland trade with Syria, Iran, India, and for the silk route. The Nile also provided Egypt with a safe and exclusive water route to Africa and the gold fields. To sustain the army Ptolemy needed experienced soldiers, the famed Macedonian hoplites. These could be obtained in Greece but at a high price. Ptolemy enticed many Greek recruits into military service with the promise of land grants. In this manner the Ptolemies managed to meet their military manpower requirements for the next two centuries. Under these buoyant economic conditions Alexandria became a world-class city and center of trade, science, and learning, as well as the capital of Egypt. Within a century of its founding Alexandria was the greatest city of the known world. By the time of Augustus, what had begun as a small port had a population of perhaps one million. (10)

The socio-economic system imposed by Ptolemy I worked well for about a hundred years until it succumbed to the pressure of Egyptian numbers and the inertia of ancient habits and practices. The number of Greeks was never sufficiently large to govern Egypt without a heavy reliance upon Egyptian priests and officials. This reliance only increased as the economy and society became more complex. Greeks preferred to live in Alexandria or the handful of urban settlements, leaving life in the vast rural hinterland and farming estates in the hands of Egyptian officials. The gradual reencroachment of Egyptian practices was already evident by 217 B.C.E. when Ptolemy IV met Antiochus III at Raphia with an army comprised mostly of native Egyptians and carried the day. The Greek population of Egypt could no longer provide the military manpower to defend the country and were now dependent upon Egyptian soldiers.

The battle of Raphia marks the beginning of a nationalist revival in Egypt and a loosening of Greek controls. Official records show that during this time land grants to Greeks almost came to a stop replaced with grants to Egyptians or joint Egyptian-Greek tenants. Intermarriage increased, and even the Greek language gave way to barbarizing influences until, by the end of the period, the official language of Egypt was once again Egyptian heavily influenced by Greek words. Greeks took to the custom of embalming their dead, and the ancient practice of brother-sister marriage, always rare and once confined only to Egyptian royalty, became so common among Greeks as to be embarrassing. (11) So thoroughly had Egyptian culture reasserted itself that by the end of the Ptolemaic period Greeks who had graduated from the gymnasium, that most Greek of all social institutions, marked their graduation with oaths to Egyptian gods! (12)

Nowhere was the evidence of Egyptianization clearer than under Ptolemy V, who by 195 B.C.E., had managed to lose much of the old Ptolemaic empire to

Antiochus and separate Egypt from the rest of the Greek world. Egypt now turned inward, with the result that the Greek kings began to think of themselves as Egyptian pharaohs. Ptolemy V, the proud heir of Macedonian kings, had himself crowned at Memphis by Egyptian priests in the manner of the pharaohs. The kings that followed spent fortunes restoring the old Egyptian temples and building new temples to the old gods at Dendera, Edfu, Kom, Ombo, and Philae, and taking for themselves the traditional royal Egyptian titulature of the pharaohs. Any pretense of worship of Greek gods was abandoned, and the traditional Egyptian priesthood once more regained its exalted position as purveyor of the official state religion. The worship of Osiris became even more widespread. When Caesar landed in Egypt he found a priesthood that was as powerful as it had ever been in the last thousand years and an Osiran faith that was more vigorous than ever. The Hellenization of Egypt, the great ideal of Alexander and Ptolemys, had failed. It seems beyond question that the gods, theology, and philosophical ideas of the Greeks made but scant impression upon the Egyptians. What had begun as a Greek ruling class in the end had been swallowed up by Egyptian culture so thoroughly that even the descendants of the first Greek kings went to their graves believing that only an Egyptian god, Osiris, could save them from the dust.

The survival of traditional Egyptian theology and religious practice during the Hellenistic period in Egypt was due to a turn of events brought about by Ptolemy I himself. From Ionia to Libya the Greek king ruled over an empire of different peoples who had little in common except the presence of Greek troop garrisons to keep them in line. Within Egypt itself the disparities of Greek and Egyptian culture posed a genuine threat to the Greek ability to govern peacefully. Ptolemy I may have been influenced by Alexander's thinking in trying to come to grips with the same problem when the latter sought to use Greek culture—the things of the *Hellenes*, thus, Hellenism—to bind his multi-cultural empire together. Ptolemy hit upon the idea of creating a common deity that all could worship and making it the official god of the imperial realm. Thus was born Serapis.

Even before Alexander's time there had been Greek colonies in Egypt comprised of mercenaries and merchants in the service of the Egyptian king. One of the largest of these colonies was at Memphis. The Greeks in Memphis came into contact with the flourishing funerary cult of the Osirified sacred Apis bull worshipped under the Egyptian name of *Usar-Hape*. The theology of *Usar-Hape* was identical to the Osiran faith, and the Memphis cult was but a local variant of the worship of Osiris where local gods such as Apis were joined with the great Osiris to raise the prestige of the local god. The Greek community in Memphis adopted the Egyptian Osiris as their own god, giving him the Greek name *Osorapis*, a

combination of Osiris and Apis. (13) The other deities of the Osiran circle, especially Isis, Horus, and Anubis, were added to the worship of Osorapis. By the
time of Ptolemy I, Greek worship of the cult of Osorapis was well established and
a large temple to him had been constructed in Memphis. (14) After a visit to the
Memphis temple Ptolemy I chose Osorapis to be the common god for the peoples of his empire.

To formulate the theology of the new god Ptolemy chose Timotheus, a Greek,
and an Egyptian priest and historian, the infamous Manetho, who had been born
at Sebennytus near the famous shrine of Isis. Timotheus was a Greek priest from
Athens from a family of sacerdotal settlers in Egypt. Each of these men was to act
as the theological representative of his people and write the theology to be attributed to the new national god. Manetho must have wielded the greater influence
in this task since the theology of the new god was indistinguishable from the theology of the Osiran faith making the official state god of the Ptolemies a thinly-
disguised copy of the traditional Egyptian Osiris. The Osiran theology of resurrection, eternal life, and a judgement beyond the grave, beliefs already more than
two millennia old in Egyptian theology, were attributed to the new national god
of the Greeks. Ptolemy gave the new god the name of Serapis and ordered a
statue of him made. The statue was fashioned by the Greek craftsmen of Sinope
on the northern shore of modern Turkey and transported to Alexandria where a
new temple, the *Serapeum*, was constructed for it by the architect Parmeniscus.
Later, under Ptolemy III, another larger temple was built.

Serapis appeared in the form of a traditional Greek god. He appeared with
luxuriant curly hair and a long beard, dressed in a cloak of Greek fashion. Seated
upon a throne, Serapis was represented leaning on a long staff which he held in
his left hand while his right hand rested upon a triple-headed Cerberus lying at
his feet. (15) The official language of Serapis' liturgy was Greek, although we
know that it was written mostly by Manetho. (16) We may safely surmise that
when the liturgy was pronounced in the Egyptian temples it was in Egyptian. To
the Egyptian mind the new god was not new at all, but the familiar Osiris who
had long comforted Egyptians with the promise of resurrection and eternal life.
In his effort to find a symbol of common loyalty for Egyptians and Greeks,
Ptolemy I had established Osiris and his Egyptian theology, albeit in Greek form,
as the official deity and religion of the empire. Within a few years a theology that
had remained extant but confined to the borders of Egypt for more than two millennia spread beyond Egypt to the entire Mediterranean world bringing with it
new theological ideas.

Isis was now officially established as the consort of Serapis and her cult spread more quickly and further abroad than the cult of Serapis himself. The worship of Isis, the embodiment of the promises of resurrection and eternal life, eventually eclipsed the worship of Serapis and even Osiris himself. The theological developments that had been emerging for a millennium within Egyt now came to fruition. Osiris, originally the god of the dead, had finally become the god of the living. It was Osiris to whom Egyptians now offered their prayers for intervention in the affairs of this world. (17) The expansion of the cult of Osiris-Isis with its promise of eternal life eclipsed the worship of Re himself. The personality of the solar Re became more and more absorbed by Osiris until the powers of Re were completely identified with Osiris. Even the name of Osiris was now written within the hieroglyph of the sun-disk instead of the usual image of the eye of Horus. (18)

The worship of Re almost disappeared during the Ptolemaic period. Osiris, Isis, and Horus were now one god in trinitarian form who possessed the power to affect men's lives while they lived and after they died. The old distinction between man living and dead was abandoned in favor of a singular human existence shared by all men and overseen by a single god at all times. By the end of the Ptolemaic period the monotheistic tendencies of Egyptian religion had fully developed into a genuine trinitarian monotheism.

Horus, too, underwent a change in status, power, and function. Horus, the son of god, became more than the good son, the epitome of filial devotion that he had been in the original Osiris myth. Now that Osiris was the god of the living and could be petitioned by the faithful for help in dealing with the cares of this world Horus acquired the position of intermediary and intercessor with the godhead, his father Osiris, on behalf of the "children of men." (19) It was Horus who, in the original myth, led the deceased into the presence of his father and urged justice for all "who are true of voice." The idea of the son of god interceding with his father on behalf of the living and dead was a new idea in Egyptian theology, and was a consequence of the transformation of Osiris into a god of the living. The notion that the common man had a "friend at court" must have been very attractive to the average Egyptian, and one can easily imagine him praying to Horus for his intercession. Christians regularly pray to God the Son for help in influencing the will of God the Father, making the analogy of Horus with Jesus difficult to avoid.

Among the most important developments of Egyptian religion during the Ptolemaic period was the re-emergence of the idea that man could establish a personal relationship with god, and that personal piety was an important element in the moral worthiness of the individual. As early as the twelfth century B.C.E. Egyptian theologians had arrived at the conclusion that Re was concerned with all his creatures. By the ninth century this idea has been extended to include the need for man to develop a devotional spirit based in a personal relationship with god. These ideas influenced the broader ethical strains of political and social justice that emerged at the end of the Feudal Age so that personal piety and social ethics were now joined as functions of one another. The result, Breasted notes, "culminated in the profoundest expression of the devotional religious spirit ever attained by the men of Egypt." (20) God and man were now joined in the achievement of moral development in this life. God looked over his people and expected justice, mercy, and compassion of all men. A prayer written by a scribe of Thebes at this time expressed this sense of moral connectivity.

> *"Who cometh to the silent, who saveth the poor, who giveth breath to every one*
>
> *he loveth, give to me thy hand. Save me, shine upon me, for thou makest my*
>
> *sustenance. Thou art the sole god, there is no other. Even Re, who dawneth in*
>
> *the sky, Autum maker of men, who heareth the prayers of him who calls to him,*
>
> *who saveth a man from the haughty, who bringeth the Nile for him who is*
>
> *among*
>
> *them, who leadeth…for all men, when he riseth the people live. Their hearts*
>
> *live when they see him, who giveth breath to him who is the egg, who maketh the*
>
> *people and the birds to live, who supplieth the needs of the mice in their holes,*
>
> *the worms and insects likewise."* (21)

For the first time in Egyptian thought the human conscience was clearly focused and fully emancipated. The moral equation was now complete, and prayer became a form of inner revelation, a personal experience through which man attained and understood what god wishes him to do so that he might become a good person.

It is obvious that an emphasis upon personal piety and prayer as the means for individual theological and moral development would serve to weaken the influence of the Egyptian national priesthood that had, by the 10th century B.C.E., achieved great power over the governmental apparatus. The movement toward personal piety and individual conscience had been restrained by the power of the Egyptian vatican as it imposed a formalistic sacerdotalism upon Egypt that lasted until the coming of the Ptolemies. The idea, however, did not die, and in the 10th century we find it again, this time in secular writings, by one Amenemope. The *Wisdom of Amenemope* was a treatise on ethics and moral development written by an Egyptian and falls within the two millennia-long tradition of Egyptian "wisdom literature." Where others argued that personal piety was virtuous because of the fear of death and post-mortem judgement, Amenemope suggested that the consciousness of god and the relationship that man established with god through his conscience and inner piety was decisive for the development of moral worthiness. For Amenemope, the inner voice that man hears in prayer is his conscience, and listening to it is essential to living a morally worthy life. The empty ritual, magic, and ceremony that marked the Egyptian sacerdotal state were of little value to the development of one's moral conscience. (22)

The wide-spread acceptance of the idea of individual conscience achieved through personal piety would have to await the end of the sacerdotal state during the Ptolemaic period. In the meantime Amenemope's ideas spread beyond Egypt where they found acceptance in Israel. The *Wisdom of Amenemope*, we can be fairly certain, was translated into Hebrew early on, most probably before the Bible itself was compiled. (23) Its main themes are clearly reflected in the Hebrew *Book of Proverbs*. It seems likely that while the idea of individual conscience remained unexploited in Egypt for almost a millennium, it may have affected the development of ethical thinking among the Jews of Israel during that time. It is also likely that it was the stimulus of these ideas, along with the independent contributions of Jewish thinkers, that provided the impetus for Jews to move away from their traditional Mosaic apodictic concept of ethical responsibility toward one that was more casuistic in nature.

Ptolemy I's adoption of a native Egyptian religion albeit in Greek form as the official religion of the empire had the effect of weakening the institutional power of the Egyptian sacerdotal priesthood of Amun-Re and focusing religious worship upon the theological doctrines identified with Osiris. At the same time the ethical thinking of Greek philosophy was given full sway with the consequence that when the Egyptian priesthood regained its power a century later, there was no turning back to the sterile ritualistic expressions that had come to characterize Egyptian religious practices over the previous centuries. Instead the priests abandoned Re and affirmed Osiris as the one true god and endorsed his theology! The idea of personal piety as the means to a life of moral worth made most sense within the context of the Osiran doctrines of resurrection and judgement, and the old ideas burst forth with new life. The formalization of the Egyptian religion under Ptolemy provoked a widespread turning toward personal piety that soon spread all over the Hellenistic world. (24)

The cult of Isis as the goddess most responsible for resurrection and insuring a fair judgement spread quickly. The attraction of this old theology in new form can be explained on two grounds. First, the "new" religion possessed the power to do what no Greek or Roman religion of the time could do, and that was the power to console. The gods of the Romans and Greeks, as well as those of the other cultures of the Near East, promised man nothing. The gods did as they wished to men with little regard for justice, mercy, or compassion. Human fate was completely out of human hands. Isis, by contrast, promised life eternal and a fair judgement of the accounting of men's moral lives as the way to achieve it. To be sure man often was forced to endure injustice in this life. But even the lowest peasant or craftsman could hope that one day justice would be done for him. Just as Osiris had comforted the lowest of Egyptians for millennia with these same promises, now it was Isis who promised justice and eternal life to the peoples of the Mediterranean.

Second, the ability to establish a relationship with god and to guide one's life by the insights learned through prayer appealed strongly to the Greek and Roman sense of personal and social ethics. Personal piety meant that man was ultimately responsible for his own moral fate and, by implication, the good or injustice of a society was the proper work of man. The fact that eternal life required a life of ethical conduct on this earth was extremely popular with Greek philosophers and Roman ethicists who had always held that proper conduct was vital to man's human development. It was the idea of a personal god and man's relationship with him, when tied to the idea of an afterlife and a fair ethical judgement beyond the grave, that was so appealing to the Greek and Roman world. The power to console supported man's need to hope, and together they gave life on this earth meaning, something which no Greek or Roman religion of the day could do. When this idea was expressed in the form of another "new" creed, Christianity, it conquered the Western world.

There is evidence that the first worship of Isis outside of Egypt preceded its formal adoption by Ptolemy I. The first trace of Egyptian gods being worshiped in Greece is found near the end of the 4th century B.C.E. in Pireaus where Egyptian traders visiting Greece on business established a small shrine to Isis. Other mention of the worship of Isis in Aegean towns occurs in the first years of the reign of Ptolemy I. (25) By the fourth century B.C.E. Athens itself was the center of Egyptian religion in Greece where many public and private shrines to Isis were established. The coins of Malta in the second and first century B.C.E. bear the figures of Isis and Osiris suggesting that the worship of these gods was known on that Mediterranean island. (26) The Ptolemaic connection with Sicily introduced the worship of Isis there early on. From there it spread to the other Hellenized cities of southern Italy. Monuments in the city of Catania in Sicily suggest that Catania may have been the center of Isis worship on the island. There were many temples to Isis in southern Italy, and by the second century B.C.E. these temples could be found in such important cities as Pompeii, Herculaneum, and Petueoli suggesting that the worship of Isis was at least as common as that of native Italian gods. (27)

Isis conquered Rome itself. A group of Isis' priests, the Pastophori, was installed in Rome during the time of Sulla, and in 43 B.C.E. the young Octavian decreed that a new temple dedicated to Isis should be built in Rome. Despite attempts to repress the cult, it continued its spread in Rome and throughout the empire. Later Augustus tried to remove the cult from Rome because Isis had been the goddess of his enemy, Cleopatra. In 19 C.E. Tiberius deported the Isis priesthood from Rome due to some scandal, but the cult was not hindered elsewhere in the empire where its spread continued. Tiberius himself, however, was no enemy of the Isis faith, and an inscription tells of him making a memorial to the Great Isis. He is portrayed in another dating from 23 C.E. as sacrificing to Hathor, Horus, and Isis. From the time of Claudius onward, Isis was regarded as the supreme foreign god of Rome, and Caligula, Domitian, and Caracalla all built temples to her. Isis became a favorite of Roman soldiers, and they carried her cult and established temples to her to the edge of the empire. Temples to Isis established by the legions of Rome have been found in the Danube region, Germany, and along Hadrian's Wall in Britain. (28) Isis also found faithful followers in Gaul and Spain, and Harbors of Isis were established on the Arabian Gulf and in the Black Sea. Isis held sway from Arabia and Asia Minor in the east to Portugal and Britain in the west, and shrines were hallowed to her in cities large and small: Beneventum, Piraeus, London, Delphi and Athens. (29)

Alexandria was the center of Isis worship in the Greek world, and there were forty-two temples dedicated to her worship in that city alone. (30) Unlike the gods of other nations whose formal worship was confined to specified feast days throughout the year, Isis was the only god of the ancient world to require *daily* worship rituals. Daily worship of the gods was an ancient Egyptian practice and its continuation in the form of daily worship of Isis suggests strongly that the substance of the ritual remained Egyptian and had not become Hellenized. The rituals remained unchanged through Roman times. (31) While other gods came and went in fashion, only the worship of Isis-Osiris persisted and flourished until the very end of paganism. (32)

The important consequence of the three century-long Ptolemaic rule of Egypt was the preservation of the ancient Egyptian theology of Osiris, Isis, and Horus and the establishment of that theology as the official religion of Egypt and the Ptolemaic empire. Freed after a millennium from the stranglehold of sacerdotalism, Egyptian theology was reinvigorated under the Ptolemies. The long repressed doctrine of piety based in the individual's personal relationship with a just and caring god reemerged and strongly influenced ethical thinking, even as it was added to the ancient promises of resurrection, judgement, and eternal life. The attraction of this theology for both Romans and Greeks was its promise of consolation, ethical guidance, and the eventual reward of eternal life, elements missing in the native religions of the West. The Isis theology spread throughout the Hellenistic and then the Roman world exposing large populations to the ancient Egyptian faith for the first time. So widespread and popular was the cult of Isis that by the first century B.C.E. anyone alive in Palestine and almost anywhere else in the West could hardly have been unaware of its existence, temples, rituals, and theological principles. This included that small band of Jewish reformers who became the world's first Christians.

The first evidence of the presence and worship of Isis and Horus in Palestine dates from the 9th century B.C.E. where figures of Isis-Nephthys dated at 860 B.C.E. are portrayed on an ivory plaque in the city of Samaria (Sebarte). (33) There is evidence of Isis worship in Palestine in the 6th century B.C.E. (34), and there is as well a third century B.C.E. dedication to Serapis and Isis. A separate item, the prayer of a Greek father describing Isis as the personification of the local Mother Goddess, also is present. (35) The Isis religion was probably brought to Palestine by Egyptian soldiers and merchants. It might be well to remind ourselves that the primary cultural influence on Palestine for the previous thousand years was Egyptian, and that it is not surprising that some of the major Egyptian theological ideas should been well known in Palestine. We have already seen that from the earliest times Egyptian wisdom literature influenced Hebrew thought. Even so, there is no evidence that Isis was worshipped by Jews or that Jews converted to her cult in any numbers. Indeed, Cerny has noted that there is not a single documented instance where an Egyptian god ever was adopted by the native Jewish population. (36)

Yet it remains reasonable that the worship of Isis and her theology was well-known within Palestine long before the birth of Jesus, whether or not many Jews converted to the Isis faith. It might be reasonably concluded that by the time of

Jesus the Egyptian theology of a single god, an immortal soul, resurrection, judgement beyond the grave, and eternal life, all ideas associated with the worship of Osiris for more than two thousand years and now associated with the worship of Isis, was clearly in evidence in Roman Palestine where it was observed by large numbers of Greeks, Romans, and the pagan peoples of Palestine who were more numerous at the time than the Jews.

Ptolemy I acquired Judea in 301 B.C.E. along with the cross-current of religious influences and beliefs that swirled through Israel at this time. Jews were a minority within Palestine, and in Samaria and the north Jews were hardly present at all. Sargon II of Assyria had carried off the more prosperous citizens of the area in 721 B.C.E., the famed "lost tribes" of Israel, leaving the area underpopulated. Those worshippers of Yahweh who remained were quickly submerged in a tide of Canaanite immigration and intermarriage. These same forces affected Judah, although not to the same degree. Two hundred years after Sargon, the Babylonian king Nebuchadressar II destroyed Judea and carried off its population into Babylonian captivity. Only a small number of these exiles returned a half-century later to find that many of those left behind had had their faith diluted by pagan practices. The returning Jewish community under Ezra and Nehemiah carried out a reform of Judaism by codifying its legal and religious tenets and reestablished Judaism in the south. Under Ptolemy I Samaria had reverted to paganism with little evidence of Jewish influence remaining, and Judaism was largely confined to the south. Everywhere else Palestine was thoroughly pagan. (37)

Judaism had to confront the seductive influence of Hellenism sweeping the Mediterranean world. The "gods" of Hellenism could be reached through reason while the god of the Jews could only be approached by revelation, ritual, and the study of the torah. Moreover, the reasonable "god" of the Greek philosophers—Aristotle's Unmoved Mover—was scarcely relevant to human affairs, whereas the god of the Jews was deeply involved in the moral life of men. Despite the efforts of such Jewish Hellenists as Philo Judeaus of Alexandria (30 B.C.E. to 45 C.E.), the fundamental tension between the two perspectives remained unresolved. (38) Hellenism spread quickly through Palestine, but remained mostly confined to the towns. In Galilee, otherwise a hot-bed of paganism and then, a century later, the locus of a fundamentalist form of Judaism, Hellenism strongly established itself in the cities and towns. With Hellenism came the official state religion of the Ptolemies and the cult of Isis and Osiris must have been as well-established in Galilee as it was in the other cities of Palestine.

The cultural intercourse between Egypt and Israel had been continuous for more than a millennium, and it continued without interruption during the time of the Ptolemies. As early as the 5th century B.C.E., Jews who had originally been mercenaries in Pharaoh's armies settled in Elephantine. They established a temple to Yahweh whom they worshipped along with the goddesses Aschima and Anat, they swore by the Egyptian gods, and they spoke Aramaic, the *lingua franca* of the Persian empire. (39) A large colony of Jews was also established at Memphis. Under Ptolemy I Jews came to Egypt in large numbers and some were granted the privileges of Greeks. We hear of Jewish-Egyptian marriages during this time and there were Jewish generals and officers in the military service of the king. (40) By the first century Alexandria possessed the largest Jewish colony outside of Palestine and it may have numbered almost a million. So frequent was the contact between Hellenes and Jews that Hebrew fell into disuse for all but liturgical purposes and was replaced by Greek and Aramaic. (41)

Within Israel itself the Jews were besieged by corrosive cultural influences that threatened to undermine their religion. Jews in Asia Minor and Persia, the descendants of those who did not return after the Babylonian Exile, adopted pagan rituals and gods. Given the rich pagan mix of the population, it was not surprising that the same thing occurred within Israel itself. This was, of course, Hellenistic syncretism at its best. But it also demonstrated that Jewish resistance to pagan ideas and practices was not very strong within Israel. Among the intelligentsia resistance to Hellenism remained strong, and the fight against it in intellectual circles continued. The result, as Tarn has noted, was a paradox. "Judaism by the first century was offering the strange spectacle of a system which refused to accept Greek thought while it opened its doors wide to the infinitely lower influences of the east—astrology, demonology, magic; because of these it hoped to make handmaidens for it own spirit (Yahweh), while the Greek spirit could be no handmaid." (42)

This tendency toward the magical and pagan within Judaism grew stronger during the first century of the Roman occupation of Palestine so that when "...the east came flooding back on the west in one great stream of astrology and magic, the Jew played a conspicuous part; Jewish magicians were reckoned second to none, and the Jewish exorcist was a familiar figure for centuries. The Jews had their own books of magic formulae." (43) The important point is that no area of Palestine was spared exposure to the many cults, religions, rituals, and philosophies that swept over the Hellenistic world at this time. There were all sorts of cultural and religious influences on Judaism during the period making it a far less distinct intellectual and logical creed than what the Greek influence on history has led us to believe. There was plenty of opportunity for a man like Jesus to become familiar with the ideas of these foreign cults. Given the popularity and wide dispersion of the cult of Osiris-Isis, it would have been strange if he was not.

One consequence of the stress of this cultural and religious assault upon Judaism was the emergence of a body of Jewish apocalyptic literature that reached its apex in the first century B.C.E. As if to confirm Samuel Eddy's observation that "resort to prophecy is a universal response of beaten men," (44) Jewish apocalyptic writings promised a form of mystical liberation of the Jews through the hand of god. Although some Jewish messianic texts predate this period, it was during this time that the idea of a messiah who would free Israel from its oppressors gained acceptance for the first time. For some the messiah was divine; for others he was not. Much of this literature reads like nationalist propaganda rooted in a heavenly prophetic vision and designed to attract wide appeal. The vision was strongly influenced by the magic of the East and contained elements of numerology, astrology, philosophy, and symbolism, often offering magical formulas for calculating the date of the apocalypse and recognizing its portents. (45) The *Book of Daniel, Enoch, The Apocalypse of Moses*, the *Testament of the Twelve Patriarchs*, and the *Song of Solomon*, along with the books of *Ezra* and *Baruch* were all written during this period and constitute the main apocalyptic literature. (46)

Jewish resistance to Hellenism also took the form of reasoned intellectual resistance by the Jewish intelligentsia led by the Jewish community of Alexandria. When Manetho's history of Egypt written for Ptolemy II proclaimed that Moses was a renegade heretic who led a band of lepers from Egypt, it was Jewish scholars in Alexandria who responded by translating the Bible into Greek, the language replacing Aramaic as the common language of the Mediterranean world. Philo Judaeus (30 B.C.E.-40 C.E.) argued that the doctrines of Hellenism and Judaism could be reconciled through the Platonic idea of the soul. Philo laid great stress upon the transcendence and incomprehensibility of god, but maintained that through god's grace man could be united with god in a mystical communion which he described as ecstasy, a divine rapture enjoyed by the prophets but more joyful and serene. Achieving this ecstasy was but a stage toward the soul's complete liberation from the body and reascension to god. (47)

One result of Jewish intellectual resistance in Egypt was the introduction of the synagogue which later became almost synonymous with Judaism. The earliest synagogue known to us from anywhere in the world appears in the second century B.C.E. in the town of Schedia near Alexandria. The origins of this religiosecular institution are shrouded in uncertainty, but it is probable that it came about during the later Hellenistic age. These houses of learning may have originated within the Jewish communities outside of Israel who were cut off from the

Temple and its rituals. The synagogues quickly became the focus of Jewish spiritual, intellectual, and national life, and they soon spread to Jerusalem and Palestine over the objections of the priestly elite. During Jesus' time synagogues were not centers of Judaic worship as they later became, and their influence on formal Judaism during Jesus' life was almost nil. They were places were Jewish intellectuals gathered to discuss the issues of the day and had no religious functions or certification as they came to have later. It was only after the Jerusalem temple was destroyed that the synagogue became a center for the observance of Jewish religious rituals. In the end both the apocalyptic and intellectual efforts failed to save Judaism from erosion. It was the struggle itself, first against Hellenism and then against Rome, that set the stage for revolt. And when revolt came it did so in both nationalistic and religious forms. Judaism diverged into two streams: the strict Sadducee tradition that stressed ritual purity and religious temple observance and the Pharisee tradition, more Hellenistic in tone and content, that preached a religious universalism understandable through teaching and study of the law. Both traditions vied for dominance for more than two centuries until consumed in the nationalist revolt of the Second Jewish War in 70 C.E. The consequences of the Jewish defeat were catastrophic. The Sadducees lost the temple itself. With the center of sacrifice destroyed, ritual purity never again played the important role that it had since the time of Moses. The Alexandrian Judaism that was a more inclusive and universal strain of Judaism and had attempted to reconcile itself with Hellenism was largely destroyed by the Diaspora. The result was that the struggle for Jewish religious loyalty was won by the ascendancy of an exclusive Levite Judaism which turned Judaism in upon itself. For a millennium Judaism once more became the enclave religion it had been at the beginning. (48)

Palestine was a maelstrom of religious and philosophical cross-currents that buffeted Judaism mercilessly and threatened to destroy it. The Romans were less interested in religion and philosophy than the Greeks and more interested in peace and prosperity. They harbored no hostility toward the Jews whom they thought more ethical and religiously observant than the Greeks. The Romans knew that Judaism was a religion of great antiquity and respected this. Jews had a reputation as ethical people among the Romans and were granted full religious liberty. Many Romans became "God-fearers," that is practitioners of Judaism observing all precepts except circumcision and some *mitzvot*. There is some evidence that one of the Flavian emperors may have converted to Judaism even as Constantine later converted to Christianity. (49) Though foreign rule was resented in Palestine, relationships between Romans and Jews were generally good. Elsewhere in the empire, relations were excellent. One tenth of the population of the imperial realm were Jews, and in Alexandria as much as 40 percent of the population may have been Jews. (50) After the Second Jewish War when Rome deported much of the population of Israel it did so without brutality. Jewish families and whole villages were deported together and resettled in cities throughout the empire that already had significant Jewish populations making it possible for Jewish communities to survive intact. (51) The Jewish population of the Roman empire increased after the Diaspora. In the first century of the Common Era, Palestine contained about two million Jews, Egypt a million, Syria about 750,000, and Babylonia about a million. At the end of the first century C.E., there were about 8,000,000 Jews in the world, about half living within imperial borders and the other half in client states. (52)

If the influence of Hellenism and its support of the Osiris-Isis theology were well known in the cities and towns of Palestine, we must inquire if these ideas were readily available in Galilee where Jesus was born and grew to adulthood. Was it likely that Jesus was exposed to the Osiris-Isis theology while living in Galilee? When the Seleucid monarch Antiochus Epiphanes (175-163 B.C.E.) attempted to impose Hellenism on Palestine he found a receptive audience in the cities. In the towns and villages, however, there was a fierce reaction that produced an upsurge of native religious feeling. It is from this time that we find the tendency to name Jewish children after the prophets and leaders of the Bible as an expression of religious pride. (53) Judaism in Galilee had been forced to live side-by-side with a strong pagan majority ever since Sargon II deported the ten tribes, so that by the time of Jesus the people of Galilee had not been Jewish very long. It was under the Maccabeean ruler of Judea, John Hyrcanus I, at the end of the second century B.C.E. that Galilee and the north had been detached from the Seleucids and joined with the homeland of Judah. It was Hyrcanus who issued a proclamation officially and forcefully converting the peoples of the north, including Galilee, to Judaism. (54) Probably less than half the population was affected by this forced conversion, and Galilee remained heavily paganized until long after Jesus' death. To the devout Jews of Jerusalem Galilee was "Galilee of the Gentiles," a derisive reference to the Jerusalem Jews' perception of their co-religionists as ritually impure quasi-pagan country bumpkins given to blasphemous thinking and strange behavior.

The Jews of Galilee saw themselves as fiercely devout and more pious than the Jews of Jerusalem, even as they adopted rituals and ideas from the East that were clearly pagan. The Galileean Jews were often at odds with the religious establishment in Jerusalem as a result, and their puritanical outlook led them to produce a rich crop of wandering holy men who claimed an intimate and direct relationship with god. These holy men operated as exorcists, healers, and miracle workers. (55) Like Hanina ben Dosa, a younger contemporary of Jesus, these sages claimed to be on personal terms with the almighty, performed miracles, cured the sick, heard voices, and forewarned of the coming kingdom of god. When Jesus did these things he was acting within the tradition of these holy men, and it was not a new experience for the people of Galilee. (56)

The Jewish community of Galilee in Jesus' day was radical and puritanical and surrounded by the hostile influences of Hellenism and its syncretic cults, including that of Osiris-Isis. Hengel in his *The Hellenization of Judea* makes the point that Galilee at the time of Christ was heavily Hellenized because it was encircled by major Hellenic cities. To the west and northwest lay Ptolemais, Sidon, and Tyre; to the northeast, east, and southeast were Panias, Caesaria Philippi, Hippos, and Gadara; and in the south were Scythopolis and Gaba, military settlements founded by Herod the Great. All these cities were bi-lingual in that both Greek and Aramaic were commonly used. (57) Michael Grant notes that Galilee was among the least isolated areas of Israel. Besides the Roman cities of Sepphoris and Tiberius, Galilee was criss-crossed with highly-traveled roads that led everywhere. Grant concludes that the Galileeans "had more intercourse with the external heathen than either the Judeans or the Samaritans." (58) Quoting Andrew Overman's demographic analysis of Lower Galilee, John Crossan notes in his *Historical Jesus* that Lower Galilee, an area approximately 15 by 25 miles, had many urban centers and large villages within that made the area "one of the most densely populated regions of the entire Roman empire." (59) One was never more than a day's walk from anywhere in the Lower Galilee. Unless one was a hermit, which Jesus was not, it would have been impossible to live in a village in Lower Galilee and be unaware of the influences of urbanization and its accompanying Hellenistic and Roman ideas. So it was, then, that "life in Lower Galilee in the first century was as urbanized and urbane as anywhere else in the empire." (60)

Just why Galilee should have acquired the reputation of being an isolated backwater is puzzling. Nazareth, the traditional town of Jesus' birth and the town where he was believed to have been raised, is not mentioned at all in traditional sources. The *Old Testament*, for example, provides a list of villages given to the tribe of Zebulon, but does not mention Nazareth. Josephus, who was responsible for military operations in this area during the Jewish war, does not mention Nazareth while giving the names of 45 other towns in Galilee. The Talmud refers to 63 towns in Galilee, but does not mention Nazareth. The evidence from tomb design suggests that Nazareth may not have existed before 200 C.E. (61) Small villager or not, Jesus lived in the shadow of a major urban administrative center in the middle of a densely populated area criss-crossed by highly traveled roads leading to other nearby major towns and cities, (62) all sources of Hellenistic influence and syncretic religions. The closest of these was Sepphoris, the "ornament of Galilee" and capital of Herod Antipas, was only a kilometer distant from Nazareth. Eric Myers notes in this regard "…the isolation that often is associated with the Galileean personality is…quite inappropriate when we speak of Jesus of Nazareth, who is growing up along one of the busiest trade routes of ancient Palestine at the very administrative center of the Roman provincial government." (63) It is beyond imagining, then, that Jesus could have lived in Galilee all his life and not been exposed to Hellenistic ideas and to the Osiran-Isis faith.

The temples and shrines to Isis in Palestine would have been very difficult for Jesus not to have noticed. Ritt has plotted the locations of most of the sites where evidence of Isis worship has been found. In Palestine alone there were temples to Isis at Gaza, Ashdod, Askelon, Shechem, Samaria (Herod's capital), Caesaria, Sepphoris, Dor, Ptolemais (Acco), Sidon and Tyre. (64) It is almost certain that the major Roman garrisons at Jerusalem, Caesaria, Samaria, Ptolemais, and Capernaum possessed Isis shrines, as would most of the Hellenized towns throughout the country. Unlike Judaism which required temple observance only three times a year, the Isis cult required daily worship with the first of four services beginning before dawn each day and the last ending in the evening with the temple lights burning. What with processions, hymns, and other rituals, Isis' temples were places of great and constant activity. The temples themselves were large (if we may judge by the nearly complete temple preserved at Pompeii), and had other attached buildings for temple assistants and workshops. The temples of Isis were not small rural shrines like those found amid the hills and glens of Greece. A more apt comparison would be the Catholic church compounds of the present day with their large buildings, attached rectories, schools, and convents, and where daily services are offered.

The evidence suggests that *it is beyond imagining that Jesus could have lived in the Galilee all his life and not been exposed to Hellenistic ideas including the theology and practice of the Isis faith.* Given the popularity of the Osiris-Isis cult with both Greeks and Romans of the time, given the evidence of wide-spread construction of shrines and temples to Isis throughout the Mediterranean world and in Palestine itself, given the popularity of Isis with Roman soldiers whose garrisons were scattered throughout Israel, and given the official support of the religion by the Roman political apparatus, one can be as certain as one can ever be when dealing with historical matters that Jesus was aware of the theology of Isis-Osiris. Indeed, it would have required a most remarkable effort of self-imposed isolation for him not to have been.

The analysis comes to rest on two simple points: One, that the Egyptian theological tradition as expressed in the principles of the Osiris myth had existed without major interruption for more than three millennia by the time Jesus was born and, as a consequence of the Ptolemies and Hellenism, was alive and thriving as a theological system with a wide following inside Egypt and throughout the Mediterranean world including the Palestine into which Jesus was born and raised. Two, it is almost a historical certainty that Jesus would have been aware of and exposed to the theology and rituals of the cult of Osiris-Isis in Palestine. If the evidence offered in support of these two propositions is sufficiently compelling, then any fundamental similarities found to exist between the theological systems of Osiris-Isis and Christianity may, in the absence of any other source from which the similarity may have been otherwise derived, be reasonably attributed to a knowledge of the theological system that is prior in time (Egyptian) as possessed by the formulator of the belief system that came after it (Christianity). Simply put, the theological similarities between the cult of Osiris-Isis and Christianity may reasonably be explained as a consequence of Jesus' adopting basic tenets of the Osiris-Isis theology into his belief system which later developed into Christianity.

NOTES

1. Nicolas Grimal, *A History Of Ancient Egypt* (London: Basil Blackwell, 1992), 382.

2. R.E. Witt, *Isis in the Ancient World* (Baltimore, MD: Johns Hopkins University Press, 1971, 20.

3. W.W. Tarn, *Hellenistic Civilization* (New York: Meridian Books, 1961), 178

4. F.E. Peters, *The Harvest of Hellenism* (New York: Barnes and Noble, 1996), 173.

5. Ibid., 165.

6. One of the great triumphs of Rome was that it was able to impose Roman law throughout the empire with minimal local variation.

7. Grimal, 381.

8. Peters, 169

9. Ibid., 170.

10. Tarn, 185.

11. The Romans were appalled by the practice which they considered incest and quickly put a stop to it.

12. Tarn, 105-108.

13. Jaroslav Cerny, *Ancient Egyptian Religion* (Westport, CT: Greenwood Press, 1979), 136.

14. Peters, 471.

15. Cerny, 137.

16. Peters, 472.

17. Cerny, 137.

18. Ibid., 138.

19. E.A. Wallis Budge, *Egyptian Ideas of the Afterlife* (New York: Dover Publications, 1995), 72.

20. James H. Breasted, *Development of Religion and Thought in Ancient Egypt* (New York: Harper and Brothers, 1959), 348.

21. Ibid., 150.

22. James H. Breasted, *The Dawn of Conscience* (New York: Charles Scribner's Sons, 1947), 330.

23. Ibid., 321.

24. Sigfried Morenz, *Egyptian Religion* (Ithaca, NY: Cornell University Press, 1973), 247.

25. Cerny, 138.

26. E.A. Wallis Budge, *Osiris and the Egyptian Resurrection* (New York: Dover Publications, 1973), vol. II, 286.

27. See Budge, Ibid. and Peters, 472.

28. A. Rosalie David, *The Ancient Egyptians: Religious Beliefs and Practices* (London: Routledge and Kegan Paul, 1982).174.

29. Ritt, 21.

30. Peters, 473.

31. Ibid.

32. Cerny, 139.

33. Ritt, 258.

34. E.A. Wallis Budge, *Osiris and the Egyptian Resurrection*, 285.

35. Ritt, 258.

36. Cerny, 128.

37. Michael Grant, *The Jews in the Roman World* (New York: Barnes and Noble, 1995), 16-17.

38. Tarn, 211.

39. Karen Armstrong, *A History of God* (New York: Ballantine Books, 1993), 68.

40. Tarn, 217.

41. Ibid., 218.

42. Ibid.

43. Ibid., 226.

44. Ibid., 235.

45. John Dominic Crossan, *The Historical Jesus: The Life of a Mediterranean Jewish Peasant* (San Francisco: Harper Collins, 1992), 104.

46. Peters, 324-325.

47. Ibid., 325.

48. Michael Grant, *The History of Ancient Israel* (New York: Charles Scribner, 1984), 275-276.

49. Crossan, 420.

50. Armstrong, 71.

51. Ibid.

52. Ibid.

53. Michael Grant, *The History of Ancient Israel*, 226.

54. John P. Meier, *A Marginal Jew: Rethinking the Historical Jesus* (New York: Doubleday Books, 1991), 207.

55. Michael Grant, *Jesus: An Historian's Review of the Gospels* (New York: Charles Scribner, 1977), 74.

56. Ibid., 75; see also Meier, 208.

57. Michael Grant, *Jesus: An Historian's Review of the Gospels*, 87.

58. As quoted in Meier, 294; see Martin Hengel, *The Hellenization of Judea in the First Century After Christ*, (Philadelphia: Trinity Press International, 1989), 14-15.

59. Michael Grant, *The Jews in the Roman World*, 4.

60. Crossan, 19; see also Andrew J. Overman, "Who Were The First Urban Christians? Urbanization in Galilee in the First Century," *Society of Biblical Literature Seminar Papers* 1988, edited by David J. Lull, 27. Atlanta: Scholars Press, 165-168.

61. Crossan, 19; Overman, 168.

62. Crossan, 15.

63. Sepphoris is only a day's walk from Nazareth, and it is often argued that Jesus may have obtained experience with the urbanized Hellenes of his day there, although there is no evidence that Jesus ever set foot in Sepphoris. Meier, 294. On the other hand, with his home being only a kilometer distant from the city, it is far more likely that he did.

64. See Ritt, maps on pages 56 and 264 respectively.

4

The Christian Osiris

John Crossan in his *Historical Jesus* says that recent historical research into the life of Jesus has become something of a scholarly joke. In recent years academic researchers have offered us no fewer than *seven* different interpretations of Jesus and his life. There is Jesus as a political revolutionary offered by S.G.F. Brandon (1967); as a magician by Morton Smith (1978); as a Galilean charismatic by Geza Vermes (1981); as a Galilean rabbi by Bruce Chilton (1984); as a Hillelite proto-Pharisee by Harvey Falk (1985); as a genuine Pharisee and Jewish faith reformer by Hyam Maccoby (1985); as an Essene by Harvey Falk (1985); as an eschatological prophet by E.P. Sanders (1985); and most recently Jesus as an historical personage by Michael Grant, an interpretation shared by Crossan himself. (1)

Crossan notes with a candor rare for academics that "this stunning diversity is an academic embarrassment. It is impossible to avoid the suspicion that historical Jesus research is a very safe place to do theology and call it history, to do autobiography and call it biography." (2) Be this as it may, the contention that Jesus incorporated many of the tenets of Egyptian Osiran theology into Christianity does not rest on any particular interpretation of Jesus' life. Instead, the proposition can be tested regardless of which of the lives noted above Jesus led. What is required is merely the affirmation of the following five propositions that no Jesus scholar ought to find unacceptable.

The first of these is that Jesus existed, that is someone to whom history attributes the founding of Christianity existed. Second, Jesus lived and died sometime during the Roman occupation of Palestine during the first half of the first century of the Common Era. Third, Jesus was some sort of religious activist or holy man who preached a creed that diverged significantly from traditional Judaism. Jesus was acting within the long established tradition of Galilean sages by claiming a special relationship with god, even describing it as filial. Whether or not Jesus thought of himself as divine, his description of a filial relationship with god permitted the interpretation by Jewish religious authorities that Jesus was claiming to be divine and the "son of god." The claim was seen as an attack upon the central Jewish belief in a monotheistic god. The further interpretation that as the son of god Jesus could forgive sins was interpreted as rank blasphemy since forgiveness of sin was a power reserved by Jewish theology to god himself. Fourth, for these and other reasons Jesus ran afoul of the Jewish religious establishment and was put to death by Roman executioners by crucifixion. Fifth, Jesus' teaching became the source of a theological system that was refined by others over the centuries but whose fundamental principles were already evident during Jesus' lifetime or shortly thereafter.

The focus of this chapter is upon Christ's beliefs as portrayed in the Gospels and Pauline letters insofar as they may be reasonably demonstrated to be similar, if not identical, to the premises of the theology of Osiris-Isis. The method of analysis is to compare the major premises of each theological system and then inquire if the Christian system could reasonably have come from the Egyptian. Other possible sources of theological ideas in Christianity besides Egyptian sources are Greek philosophy and the beliefs and rituals of pagan religions extant at the time.

Let us begin with the proposition that it is not unusual that we should look for the origins of Christianity *outside* the teachings of Jesus. The Christian notion that Jesus was a god who became man, who possessed a complete human nature which permitted his suffering and death to be experienced as a human person, who died and was resurrected, and who came to sit at the right hand of the godhead where he assessed the moral worthiness of men after death as a prerequisite for eternal life is so starkly similar to the myth of Osiris as to be *prima facie* identical. It is equally obvious that this story could not possibly have come from Judaism for none of the major theological premises of Christianity were incorporated into the Judaism of Jesus' day nor, for that matter, are they today. There is no denying the fact that Jesus' affirmation of the theology of the new Christianity represents an almost complete break with the Judaism of his day and not, as some would have it, a continuation of it.

Beginning with Saint Paul, Christians have gone to great lengths over the centuries to demonstrate the Jewish roots of Christianity. Maccoby suggests that this was initially due to the fact that Judaism enjoyed considerable prestige among the Romans as a creed of great antiquity whose adherents lived ethical lives. (3) The doctrine was developed later by Christian theologians that Judaism was the "older brother" of Christianity because its history and theology prefigured the life of Jesus and the coming of the new creed. (4) The validity of such a claim cannot be tested by the historian who is more likely to regard a reinterpretation of Jewish history in light of Christian theological precepts as an exercise in poetry rather than history.

Saint Paul seems not to have been very curious about these difficulties and appears to have overlooked the stark similarities that early Christianity shared with the pagan beliefs and practices of his day. Other Christian writers, however, saw them clearly enough. (5) Julian and Tertullian viewed these similarities with great alarm, and tried to explain them away. But the Pauline emphasis on Judaism as the precursor of Christianity in the face of all evidence to the contrary precluded any recognition of other sources for Christian doctrines. The consequence was that these writers had no explanation to offer, and had to content themselves with the less than convincing argument that Satan had maliciously concocted the pagan forms in the image of Christianity to lead souls astray. (6) The explanation offered here is that some fundamental tenets of Christian theology were borrowed from other extant sources, most particularly from the Osiris-Isis faith.

In the early stages of development religions do not seek to express a precise theology as much as they attempt to strengthen the ties of belief and communion and win the struggle for existence. This was surely the case in the early days of Christianity when Palestine was an area within which Egyptian, Greek, Roman, and Oriental deities and Hellenistic philosophies appeared side by side as they jostled one another for attention and survival. Some "leakage" of ideas from one "belief system" to another was inevitable. Any study of Greek and Egyptian papyri of the time reveals "that Christian and Jewish prayers, quotations, and sacred names appear cheek by jowl with their Egyptian, Greek, and Babylonian counterparts." (7) The magical papyri reveal similar spells and rituals with the basic difference being nomenclature, so that Christian magicians healed by invoking the name of Jesus while Jewish magicians did the same by invoking Yahweh. It is only after the battle for survival has been won that the new cult attempts to form itself more clearly by formulating and expounding a distinct theology. The aim is definition, and the mechanism of its achievement is the formulation of a distinct terminology through which the theology's beliefs and rituals are expressed. In a strict sense, then, the Christian creed of Jesus' time was not a proper theology at all, but a set of core beliefs that came eventually to define the new faith.

We should not expect to find these core beliefs expressed in complete form during the early days of Christianity's existence. It required centuries, as it did for Judaism and Egyptian religion, for Christian theologians to produce a more definitive theology. If the analysis is to compare Christian with Egyptian, Jewish,

Babylonian, and Hellenistic ideas extant during the first century C.E., then it must compare those Christian beliefs *as we can determine them to have been commonly understood then* rather than *as they came to be understood* after a millennium of theological embellishment by Christian theologians. It is, moreover, pointless to debate which of these early Christian beliefs were espoused directly by Jesus or which were attributed to him by his followers after his death. What is important is not what Jesus said or meant, but what early Christians *came to believe he said or meant.* It is clear enough from Paul's letters to the Corinthians, less than thirty years after Jesus' crucifixion, that the key principles of the new Christian faith were already sufficiently understood among the faithful for them to inquire of Paul what they meant. The task, then, is to enumerate the fundamental beliefs of the new faith in the same basic way that the early Christians understood them.

The fundamental beliefs of early Christianity are the following: (1) Jesus is a god who became incarnate as a human being; (2) the god-head is expressed monotheistically but in trinitarian form, that is as three distinct persons, equally divine, in one god; (3) man is possessed of an immortal soul; (4) after the death of the body, the soul rises again and lives on; (5) the moral worthiness of a man is judged by god after his death; (6) those who pass this judgement are granted eternal life. *It is the point of this analysis to demonstrate that each of these basic Christian beliefs was adopted from the beliefs of the Egyptian cult of Osiris-Isis because they are identical in both theologies and could not have come from any other source—Judaism, Greek theology or philosophy, or the Oriental religions—for the simple reason that these beliefs did not exist within any of the other sources at the time they were first evident in Christianity.* And since it ought to be clear from the previous chapters that these same beliefs originated and were developed within the body of traditional Egyptian religion millennia before the birth of Jesus, it follows that the direction of influence must have been from Egyptian theology to Christian belief and not vice versa.

Among the most compelling ideas of Christianity is the idea that Jesus was a god who became man. The incarnation of god in genuinely human form requires, to say the least, a dramatic change in the existential form of the deity carried out in a manner similar to creation in which the word of god (*logos*) became flesh (*sarx*). (8) Through this creative process the god comes to dwell completely in the body of a human being, literally the god is "made flesh." In human form the god possesses all elements of human nature, *including the ability to die.* This latter is of central importance since the suffering and death of Jesus is what gives a redemptive quality to his agony and death. Through incarnation the death of the god is given a historical quality as well, that is, it is held to have actually occurred, rather than leaving the idea of an incarnated god solely in the realm of myth.

The prospect that the incarnation and death of a god actually occurred in history provided Christianity with a powerful attraction, as did the belief that the event was held to have been witnessed by other men. The purpose of the incarnation of the god was to atone for the sins of the human race. Incarnation was required to attain this because the magnitude of the human offense against a perfect god required that the redeemer be a member of the human race which had committed the sins and that he suffer as humans would. (9) The central feature of Christianity, the redemptive death of Jesus, would be completely incomprehensible without a concept of incarnation to bring about the existential change from god to man.

Incarnation is a very sophisticated concept and is unlikely to have been developed independently and out of whole cloth by a Jewish holy man living in rural Galilee in the first century of the Common Era. Jesus' Judaism would certainly have been of no help since there is no hint in the Judaism of his time (or since) of a concept of incarnation. Greek philosophy, too, in its Hellenistic form, did not contain any such notions. Other religions of the day held that the gods could walk among men and interfere with their fates, but none thought that the gods could assume a true human nature and subject themselves to the risk of dying or being slain by men or other gods. The gods changed form superficially as in Ovid's *Metamorphoses*; that's all. The only source that could have provided early Christian thinkers with the idea of incarnation was the Egyptian theology of Osiris-Isis.

Egyptian thinkers developed the idea of incarnation more than two millennia before Jesus and it was a central principle of Egyptian theology from at least 3000 B.C.E. onward. Incarnation was the natural corollary of the manner in which the Egyptians viewed creation itself. The earliest compilation of the Egyptian version of creation occurs in the *Memphite Drama* of about 2700 B.C.E., but is commonly thought to contain ideas that were much older. Wallace Budge notes that at this time the "priests of Ptah had arrived at the highest conception of god which was ever reached in Egypt...They evolved the idea of god as a spirit, a self-created, self-sustaining, eternal, almighty mind-god, the creator of all things, the source of all life and creation, who created everything that is merely by thinking...the Word which gave expression to the thought that "came into his mind." (10)

In Egyptian theology god creates *ex nihilo,* and he does so by thinking about what he wishes to create and then uttering the name of the thing; "what the heart thought and the tongue commanded." (11) We find this same notion of creation in the *Logos* doctrine of the New Testament in the Gospel of John where he says, "In the beginning was the Word, and the Word was with God, and the Word was God...All things were made by him; and without him was not any thing made that was made." (12) In the Egyptian view all things are made by god through incarnation of the word, that is, by the spirit or idea determining a physical reality. The gods themselves also enter into their physical images and are genuinely present within them. "...So the gods entered into their bodies of every kind of wood, of every kind of stone, of every kind of clay." (13) Even the creator could become incarnate. The Memphite cult of Ptah worshiped him in the form of the sacred Apis bull that was Ptah himself as he appeared to men on earth. In the same sense that god was incarnate in Jesus and his human nature, so it was that the Egyptians believed that Ptah was incarnate in the Apis bull and its nature. It was the same with all Egyptian gods. They were present and alive within their images not symbolically *but in the flesh* in a manner that seems identical to Jesus' inhabiting, or indwelling, or assuming a human body and nature. (14)

Purely as an idea incarnation has its roots *only* in Egyptian theology appearing no where else in the Near East or in the West until it made its appearance in Christian doctrine in the first century of the Common Era. What lends further credence to the suspicion that the Christians adopted the idea of incarnation from the followers of Osiris-Isis is the parallel manner in which each religion *applied* the concept to its own theology. Jesus became man and died, as did Osiris before him. Jesus' possession of a human nature is precisely what gives his death a redemptive quality. It is Osiris' human nature and his horrible death that makes Osiris a sympathetic judge of human frailty, for only a god who has been truly human can understand how difficult it is to behave properly on this earth. Of all the gods only Osiris became human, just as Christians affirm that Jesus is the only god to have become human.

Jesus' presence on this earth was affirmed to be an historical event in the same way that Egyptian theologians affirmed that Osiris's sojourn in this life was an historical event. Finally, Jesus' life, death, and resurrection purchased the possibility of eternal life for all mankind just as in Egyptian theology it was the life, death, and resurrection of Osiris that purchased the possibility of eternal life for all men. The similarities between the manner in which the concept of incarnation is *applied* in both the Osiris-Isis and Christian theologies suggests the possibility that the central drama of Jesus' incarnation and his death may have been adopted completely from Egyptian sources. At the very least it is unlikely that the idea of incarnation found in early Christian theology was a product of original Christian thinking.

Among the Jews of Jesus' day perhaps the most controversial of Christian theological ideas was the notion that the god-head was comprised of three distinct persons, the Father, Son, and Holy Spirit, each equally divine even as they together constituted at the same time a single unified god. The doctrine of the Trinity required centuries to clarify officially. Among the most authoritative early works on the subject by a major Christian theologian was *De Trinitate* (On The Trinity) by Augustine of Hippo in the fifth century C.E. (15) During the earliest days of Christianity, however, the doctrine of the trinity was not present in such complete and specific form. Its major postulates were, however, sufficiently evident at least to Jewish theologians of the day to permit a charge of blasphemy against Jesus for his claim that he was the "son of god." Jesus' ministry paralleled that of other Galileean holy men in that he claimed a special relationship with god. That he portrayed this relationship as filial, namely like that of a son to his father, is evident by his frequent use of the word *Abba* which means father in the most intimate sense. (16) We are uncertain what Jesus meant by this. We cannot tell whether his consciousness of an intimate relationship with a supreme god amounted to a belief of his own divinity or not. What is obvious, however, is that many of those around him *believed* Jesus to be divine, that is the son of god in a literal sense, or else believed him to be claiming to be divine even while they believed he was not. Christian doctrine wasted little time in affirming that Jesus was divine.

The claim attributed to Jesus that he could forgive sins bolstered the conviction that he was claiming to be divine. In Jewish theology the forgiveness of sin is a power reserved to the singular god. It was on these two grounds, polytheism and forgiveness of sin, that Jewish theologians saw Jesus as blasphemous. When charges were brought against him, the Pharisees tell Pilate, "We have a law; and by that law he ought to die, because he has claimed to be the son of god." (17) It is important to note the seriousness with which other religions regard the Christian claim of a trinitarian god. Many modern Jewish and Muslim theologians do not regard Christianity as a monotheistic religion seeing in the affirmation of a trinitarian god the continued practice of polytheism.

Jesus' invocation of the paraclete or Holy Spirit provoked fears among Jewish theologians that he was affirming yet a third person within the god-head. The belief in a single omnipotent god had precluded the Jews from developing a doctrine of evil. From the time of the *Blessing of Moses* (18) the Jews had believed that Yahweh alone was responsible for all things, including the evil that befell man.

To be sure Yahweh could employ devils, demons, and spirits to do his bidding, but these creatures were hirelings with no independent power. When the Jews returned from their exile in Babylon (5th century B.C.E.) they brought with them the Babylonian idea of a supernatural being who causes evil. They called this being "Satan," from the root word "to oppose." Satan was not yet regarded as an opponent of Yahweh and could only act with Yahweh's permission. By the time of the *Book of Chronicles* (250 B.C.E.), however, the attribution of evil to Satan himself became well established within the Jewish apocalyptic literature if not the traditional mainstream. (19) The perception of Jesus' theological enemies that he spoke of the Holy Spirit as an entity co-equal with the father and son was horrifying in that it appeared to be incorporating a powerful evil spirit within the god-head.

In the affirmation of a trinitarian god by the Christians we see the incorporation of a theological idea that is found nowhere else except in the traditional religion of Egypt. Judaism was rigidly monotheistic, and the paganisms of the day were eclectically polytheistic, so that neither of these religious influences produced the theologically radical concept of trinitarianism. Nor can Hellenistic philosophy have been the source. Hellenistic religious syncretism permitted the idea that there was an apparent theological unity evident in the world. Behind the differences all people were essentially worshipping the same single god. But this was not trinitarianism. The idea that there might be a tri-partite entity united in a governing singularity was first broached in Greek philosophy by Plotinus (205-270 C.E.) in the second century in his affirmation in the *Enneads* of the existence of "three divine hypostases" which he identified as the One, the Intelligence, and the Soul. This idea was advanced to explain the *natural* not the *theological* universe and came too long after Jesus' death to have influenced early Christian thinking.

The only place where the notion of a trinitarian god is found at the time of Jesus is in Egypt where it had been invented and in evidence within theological thought for more than two thousand years. The idea of a trinitarian god-head emerged as an answer to the Egyptian perception that behind the complexity of the world there was a unifying singularity to which all existence could be attributed. The cults of many gods from time immemorial were only variations in the worship of a single god who often hid himself from mankind. Egyptian theologians conceived of the trinity as a way of incorporating the worship of many gods into the reality of a single god without threatening the ancient validity of local gods. In this way the greatest gods of Egypt were often assembled in trinities that incorporated the traditional god of a major city or region. The oldest known

Egyptian trinity is that of Ptah, Osiris, and Sokaris, the latter being the local god of Memphis. (20) In an Egyptian trinity, like the Christian trinity, the unity of the parts constitutes a genuine singularity, that is one god. Each of the "persons" within the Egyptian and Christian trinity has an independent existence, is distinct in nature, is equally divine, and has its own identity even as each is part of the singular monotheistic unified god at the same time. (21) The genuine singularity of the unified god was reflected in Egyptian semantics where the god-head was always referred to by the singular pronoun, He, taking the majestic form. (22)

Over the centuries, of course, the incorporation of a different local god with the major deity would occur. During the New Kingdom, for example, the power of the warrior princes of Thebes elevated their local god, Amun, to inclusion into the trinity of Re-Amun-Osiris. Anyone visiting a temple of Isis in, say, the Roman city of Sepphoris during Jesus' day would have found the trinity of Serapis-Isis-Horus worshipped there. Not only had the Egyptian idea of a trinitarian god survived into Jesus' time, but its ritualistic expression was a common, indeed daily, occurrence within the Palestine of Jesus' life. Had the early formulators of Christianity wished for whatever reason to incorporate trinitarianism into their theological beliefs it would have been a simple thing to do. Those familiar with the Osiris-Isis cult would have immediately recognized the idea. Trinitarianism was not an original theological innovation of early Christian thinkers but an adoption of a very ancient Egyptian theological idea that was readily available for the taking during the time and in the place where Jesus lived out his ministry.

The Christian idea of the soul is closely bound up with resurrection and eternal life since it is the soul, not the earthly body, that rises after death and lives forever. The central attributes of the Christian soul are that it is the animating force of human life and is of divine origin, immaterial, and individually immortal. The soul constitutes the essence of a human personality. Over the centuries these concepts became much more refined and elaborate as the result of theological analysis by Christian thinkers. In Jesus' day, however, this level of refinement was not yet present. Even when expressed it its simplest forms, the followers of Jesus had some difficulty grasping the idea of an immortal soul. Even Saint Paul had great difficulty convincing the Corinthians of the immortality of the soul. At its most basic, however, most Christians believed the soul to be of divine origin and was immortal. Brandon describes this Christian perspective. "Belief in the soul's superiority to the body, by virtue of its divine origin and intrinsic immortality, thus became a fundamental tenet of Christianity. It was basic to the whole scheme of salvation; and it inspired the abiding Christian disposition to asceticism, whereby the soul is exalted and the body despised." (23) In searching for the source of the Christian idea of a soul the key concepts are the soul's divine origin and personal immortality. Virtually all religions of the Near East understood that there was some principle of animation that breathed life into all creatures. But only the Egyptians saw the soul as a purposeful creation of god that was individually immortal.

Babylonian religions recognized that humans possessed a principle of animation (*napistu*) whose origin was attributed to nature, not god. Mesopotamian theologians did not see this soul-like entity as immortal. Yet, they maintained that the principle of life did not disappear entirely at death. They recognized that death brought a terrible change to the living person and transformed him into some sort of ghost or *etimmu*, a mere shade or insubstantial wraith of the person's former self. These entities dwelt in the *kurnugia* or land of no return "where dust is their food and clay their substance…where they see no light and dwell in darkness," as the *Legend of Gilgamesh* tells us. (24) It is important to understand that this is not the equivalent of Hell, for *all* men, great and small, good and bad, ended up here. This quasi-human dreary afterlife is merely the description of a natural process that all living creatures undergo as a consequence of their material natures. The central qualities of the Christian soul, divine origin and personal immortality, were completely absent in the Babylonian religions of Jesus' time and before.

Had Jesus turned to Judaism for the concept of an immortal soul he would have found that Jews never entertained the idea. The Jewish idea of the soul is strongly parallel to that of the Babylonian religions and since Moses was silent on the issue, it is at least possible that Jewish post-Exilic thinking on the subject may have been shaped by the Jews' exposure to the theologies of Babylon during the Exile. The Hebrew notion of the soul is first mentioned in *Genesis* were God creates man and breathes life into him so that Adam becomes "a living soul." Egyptian theologians used these same words to describe the *ba* when it changes its nature and becomes "a living soul." *Genesis*, of course, is a legend of Mesopotamian origin and was not incorporated into the Bible until about 800 B.C.E., or right around the time of the establishment of the first known Isis temple at Samaria in Palestine.

Soul in Hebrew is *nephesh* and connotes the joint physical and psychic elements in man. It is very similar in meaning to the Babylonian *napistu*, and its physical character can be seen in its association with blood, the life substance, that was thought to drain away from the body at death. The possession of *nephesh* does not in any way define or distinguish man from other humans or from other creatures. All living things possess *nephesh*. Once again the parallel with the Babylonian *napistu* is evident. There is absolutely no sense in Judaic theology that the soul of an individual is special in any way, and certainly not that it is of divine origin or immortal. (25) Although Elijah used the term *ruach* to describe the soul, the term does not mean soul at all, but rather a sense of one's breath or spirit. As in Babylonian theology, death brought with it a separation of the body from its life principle. Probably during the Exile the idea grew up that the person's "shade" or shadow lived on underground in a partial existence of his former self. For the Jews death was a natural and final event. There is no sense that personality or any significant part of man's existence was able to continue forever.

By Jesus' day the influence of Hellenism among the intellectuals of Alexandria moved some, like Philo, to accept the Platonic idea that the soul might live on beyond the grave. But such speculations of an intellectual elite in a foreign city never fully developed the idea within the context of Jewish theology. (26) Whatever influence they may have had on early Christian thinkers, if any, is impossible to discern from this distance. Even when such ideas mingled with the apocalyptic Jewish literature of the period, no doctrine of the divine origin of the soul and its immortality emerged within any body of Jewish theological thought. "The old Semitic tradition prevailed. The immortality of the soul alone was never deemed sufficient, and Jewish eschatology could only envisage a satisfactory after-life as the restoration of the whole people..." (27) when it envisaged it at all.

Because of the influence of Greek philosophy upon the *later* development of Christian doctrine, it is sometimes thought that the Christian notion of the soul was taken from the ideas of Greek philosophers, most notably Plato, that had spread through the Mediterranean world on the wings of Hellenism. But Hellenism offered no notion of a divine and personal immortal soul that could have been adopted by early Christians. From Homeric to Hellenic and even Graeco-Roman times, the Greek idea of a soul was strikingly similar to the Babylonian and Hebrew concepts.

The first expression of the Greek idea of a soul is found in the Homeric poems. The individual is seen to be comprised of three parts, the body, the *psyche*, and the *thymos*. The *psyche* was the life-giving principle located in the head while the *thymos*, located in the lungs (*phrenes*), was identical with the mind or consciousness. At death, the *thymos* perished while the *psyche* survived whereupon it was transformed into the *eidolon*, an insubstantial shade or shadow of the former living person. (28) The idea is poetically presented by Homer when Odysseus meets his dead mother, Anticleia, in Hades. He tries to embrace his mother's shade only to have his arms pass through it. Odysseus cries out, "is this but a phantom (*eidolon*)?" Anticleia replies, "....this is the way with mortals when they die: the sinews no more hold together the flesh and bones, but they are overmastered by the force of the strong burning fire, as soon as the life (*thymos*) has left the white bones, and the shade (*psyche*) hovers like a dream and flits away." (29) By Plato's time this idea had changed only slightly when the *psyche*, not the *thymos*, came to be regarded as the essential self, the seat of both consciousness and the life principle.

Plato (428-348 B.C.E) attempted to devise an idea of the soul. He affirmed the existence of a divine, unchanging reality that existed beyond the realm of the senses, a world of ideal forms that could be reached by the operations of the mind. Plato's theory of perfect forms is a very old idea, perhaps little more than the ancient pagan myth of the existence of a divine world of the gods where everything is perfect while the material world is but an imperfect "participation" of this ideal world. (30) Plato's idea is a "rational" version of this mythical divine order where, paradoxically, an old pagan myth is put to the service of monotheism. One can see at a glance how attractive this perspective would become to later Christian thinkers. The existence of a divine world of perfect forms knowable through reason became crucial to Christian monotheists as they struggled to express their conception of a singular god. The idea that ideal forms were to be found within the minds of men implied that the objects of thought were genuine realities that were active within the mind of the person who contemplated them. In this way man could possess a knowledge of god. It is thinking that permits man to reach god or even to become divinized. (31)

In Plato's view the soul existed in an elevated ethereal state. Some souls could not sustain themselves in this manner and sank down to find a resting place within men or animals of the material world where they became contaminated and entrapped. The body in which the soul finds itself is as a prison. After the body died the soul could move on to another body, perpetuating a cycle of rebirth. (32) In this sense the soul might be seen as immortal, but its immortality appears to be nothing more than a philosophical "fact," for its immortality has no implications for humans that are not shared by animals nor any that are shared by the gods. There are no implications for the divine. It is more correct to say that Plato's soul is *indestructible* rather than immortal. The idea that the soul at death moves from one individual to another is eerily similar to the Hindu doctrine of the transmigration of souls.

The popularity that Plato's idea later acquired among Medieval Christian theologians was not evident during Plato's lifetime or later Hellenistic times. The idea of an immortal soul was never a view held by more than a handful of minor

Greek philosophers during the Hellenistic period. The majority view of the soul remained pessimistically Homeric. There was no imputation of divine origin or personal immortality that could be derived from any of the extant Greek philosophical doctrines of the Hellenistic period. Hellenism's leading philosophers generally did not believe the soul to be immortal. Lucretius in his *De Rerum Natura* offers no fewer than twenty-eight arguments against the idea of an immortal soul. The Stoics were materialists which makes the idea of an immortal soul problematic. The Skeptics notoriously withheld judgement. It is unlikely that early Christian believers adopted the idea of an immortal soul of divine origin from the Hellenistic thinkers of the day.

It was only in Egypt that Christians could have discovered their conception of the soul. From time immemorial Egyptian theologians had affirmed that the soul was of divine origin, that it was fashioned by god "on the potter's wheel" and infused into man at birth. It was only in Egypt that Christians could find the idea that the individual soul was immortal and lived on after death to make its way back to its creator for judgement and eternal life. Neither of these concepts adopted by early Christian thinkers can reasonably be attributed to any other source at the time when they were first adopted. The reasonable conclusion is that they were taken directly from the Osiris-Isis theology.

The most important idea of the new Christian doctrine, one requiring belief in personal immortality, was resurrection, the belief that man would rise from the dead and continue to live forever. While stories about Jesus' resurrection began appearing almost immediately after his death, the first written statement of the new Christian belief appeared about twenty years after the crucifixion in a letter by Paul to the Corinthians. In trying to explain what Christians believed in this regard Paul says "…that Jesus died for our sins, according to the scriptures; that he was buried; that he was raised to life on the third day, according to the scriptures, and that he appeared to Peter, and afterwards to the Twelve." (33) Because Jesus gained salvation for all persons by his death, Christian resurrection was available to all as individuals. It was, moreover, immediate, that is to say it did not require some apocalyptic final judgement to bring it about. The words attributed to Jesus during his crucifixion to the thief next to him that "on this day you will be with me in paradise," imply that when people died they were resurrected immediately. During Paul's life the idea of resurrection was strongly held to mean that the body would be resurrected as well. Later, this belief also became part of the formalized doctrine of Christianity.

To Babylonians and Jews who believed that death destroyed the human personality leaving only a disfigured partial self, such an idea was incomprehensible.

As Morton Smith has remarked, the idea of resurrection could not have been derived from rabbinic Judaism because "no such belief is known to have been held by any rabbi of this time." (34) Greek philosophers believed the soul to be imprisoned in the body as in a tomb. The thought of keeping the soul trapped within a body for eternity was ridiculous to the Greek mind. Once again we see early Christianity adopting an idea that could not have been taken from the Babylonian or Jewish religions of the day nor from the Hellenistic influences that swirled around the new Christian cult. It was an idea that Hellenistic Greeks found equally outrageous. *Acts*, xvii, 16-24 tells of Paul being mocked by the Greeks in Athens when he attempted to explain the Christian promise of resurrection to them.

In Greek the phrase "resurrection of the dead" is *anastasis nekron*, literally "standing up of corpses." (35) Paul's use of the phrase is intriguing for it describes exactly what the Egyptian funeral ritual prescribes to achieve resurrection. Once the embalmers had prepared the body for entombment, the coffin was brought to the mouth of the tomb. There the coffin was stood up on its feet so that the Egyptian priest could perform the ceremony of "the opening of the mouth." The priest touched the five senses—ears, nose, mouth, eyes, and hands—with an aziz revivifying them and bringing the body back to life. Christians will immediately recognize the touching of the senses as similar to the anointing of the senses in baptism thereby bringing them to the "new life in Christ." Why would Paul use a phrase that would evoke the Egyptian ritual in the minds of his Greek listeners? One reason may have been that Corinth, like most Greek cities of the Peloponnese, possessed temples to Isis-Osiris that dated from pre-Christian times. The Corinthians would have been familiar with the Osiran doctrine of resurrection, and Paul was simply using familiar language to explain the Christian version of the well-known Egyptian doctrine to his audience.

Only in Egypt do we find the idea of resurrection after death based on *personal* immortality, where it had already become a central tenet of the Osiris-Isis cult more than two thousand years before Jesus was born. Resurrection is among the earliest principles of Egyptian religion dating at least from the third millennium B.C.E.. Resurrection was held by the Egyptians to be the logical consequence of incarnation. Ptah, for example, was incarnated in the material form of the Apis bull. When the Apis bull died, the soul of Ptah left the body and was incarnated in the next Apis bull. That death was followed by the continuation of life was clear from the tombstones of the graves of the sacred bulls which read "Apis the Living." The same idea is found in Christian practice whenever a petitioner prays to Jesus as "the living god." (36) Over the centuries the privilege of resurrection gradually was extended to include all humans, and it became a core belief in the theology of Osiris-Isis. Both Christian and Osiris-Isis theologies are inexplicable without it. (37)

There is, however, another source that might have provided a notion of resurrection to the early Christians, and that is the tradition of apocalyptic Judaism. By the time of the Maccabean wars (165 B.C.E.), some Jews came to believe that the dead, complete with their bodies, would rise again once god had returned, judged the world, and punished all but the righteous. These righteous Jews, called the Remnant, would then enjoy eternal life. This idea is the closest that Judaic thought ever came to a notion of resurrection, and it has its roots in the eschatological literature of the 2nd century B.C.E., most particularly the *Book of Daniel*.

This body of radical nationalist literature was a reaction to the long suffering of the Jews under foreign rule, and conceived the idea of a messiah who would come to cure the evil of this world. The messiah was to be a great man, but in no sense was he thought to be divine. His coming was an indication that the end of the world was near by God's judgement. It is only after the messiah completes his earthly work and frees Israel from her enemies that God comes to earth and wreaks havoc upon the unjust, saving only the Remnant of devout Jews. Those virtuous Jews already dead would be brought back to life along with their physical bodies. Where they went, then, is unclear. The sinful were either slain or went to the old *Sheol* which, as described in the books of *Enoch* and *Ezra*, had now been transformed into a place called *Gehenna*, originally the site of the city dump of Jerusalem. The *Sheol* was transformed into a place of flaming torment having various divisions to which the dead were assigned according to their sins. (38)

The idea of *resurrection by apocalypse* is first found in the *Book of Daniel* written in 167-164 B.C.E. by an unknown author in Aramaic and Hebrew. It is a collection of popular legends about a Jew named Daniel living at the Babylonian court at a time before the Jews returned from Exile. Daniel's tomb can be seen to this day in the Iraqi city of Kirkuk. Daniel introduced the idea of the coming of god who will liberate the Jews and punish their enemies. (39) Daniel's contribution to the onset of Jewish thinking about resurrection is found in the following passage: "Many of those who sleep in the dust of the earth will awake, some to everlasting life and some to the reproach of eternal abhorrence." (40) Along with the apocalyptic vision this idea in one form or another can be found, often only implicitly, among other books of the apocalyptic literature. The books that are closest in time to Jesus are the *Testament of Moses* dating from Maccabean times, the *Song of Solomon* written around 48 B.C.E., and the *Book of Enoch* written sometime in the last half of the first century B.C.E. (41) Is it likely, then, that the early Christians, themselves Jews, obtained the idea of resurrection from their own apocalyptic literature?

Probably not, for the simple reason that the idea of *apocalyptic resurrection* is quite different from the Christian concept. The apocalyptic resurrection of Daniel is *communal* and does not apply to *individuals* per se. Resurrection is not connected with the destinies of individual persons but with the destiny of a nation where only the Jewish devout are freed from the gentiles by God. Apocalyptic resurrection embodies an idea of *national* salvation and vindication occurring as a singular act of god's power and justice and does not constitute a theology of individual justice, morality, judgement, or salvation. Apocalyptic resurrection requires the end of history; the judgement of the dead and living is a singularity, not a continuous reality. (42) By contrast Christian resurrection, like Osiran resurrection, addresses the salvation of the *individual*, not the nation, and does not require the eschaton or the coming of god. Christian resurrection is immediate and personal, not apocalyptic and national. And it is promised to all men, not just a religious elect. (43)

The differences between the apocalyptic and Christian versions of resurrection are sufficient to disqualify the former as the source of the latter in early Christian thinking. Moreover the *Book of Daniel* was not adopted into the Hebrew theological cannon of the Prophets in Jesus' time because the prophecies contained within it were considered by some to be dangerous and bordering upon the heretical. (44) Some Christian biblical scholars reject this view arguing that Daniel is the precursor of Christian thinking on the idea of resurrection pointing to Paul's affirmation that the dead will be "gathered up" or Mathew's assertion that "nations" not individuals will be judged as evidence that early Christian views of resurrection were in fact communal and not immediate. The argument is unconvincing.

One idea that may have been adopted from *Daniel*, however, is the notion that the previously righteous dead would somehow be included in resurrection. In the Christian version Jesus descends into Hell for three days prior to rising from the dead. This is interpreted as extending the promise of resurrection to the righteous dead who, until the crucifixion, had no hope for it. On the face of it the idea seems to have been taken from Daniel. There is, however, a much older Egyptian source for the idea. It is very similar to the ancient belief that Osiris and Re descend into the world of the dead each day at the setting of the sun to tend to the souls in the underworld and lead the righteous among them to eternal life. (45) Later, Christians adopted the apocalyptic notion of a Second Coming, although given resurrection and judgement as immediate occurrences upon one's death it is unclear what purpose a Second Coming would serve.(46) If it is argued, nonetheless, that the Christians adopted resurrection from apocalyptic Judaism, one could still inquire as to how such a radical idea found its way into the apocalyptic literature in the first place. In this regard it may be helpful to remember that the Egyptian influence on Jewish religious and ethical thinking was already a long established fact with much of Egyptian wisdom literature making its way into Jewish texts long before Daniel.

The emergence of the apocalyptic texts coincides with a general increase in Jewish-Egyptian cultural contact. During this time a number of Jewish colonies were established in Egypt, the Jewish intellectuals of Alexandria were already famous, Jewish immigration to Egypt increased, and many Jews entered the service of the Egyptian government including soldiers and generals. Under these conditions it would have not been unreasonable for Egyptian ideas on immortality and resurrection to have had some influence upon the apocalyptic authors. It is almost beyond comprehension that Jewish thinkers would have developed the idea of resurrection on their own, an innovation that would have required the abandonment of Jewish ideas about death and the soul maintained since the time of Moses. However it came about, apocalyptic notions of the soul and resurrection are further from Christian conceptions than are the ideas of soul and resurrection found in the theology of Osiris-Isis. The similarity of *meaning* and *application* argue for the source having been Egyptian.

The Christian belief in judgement after death as a prelude to eternal life necessarily depends on a belief in the prior theological tenets of an immortal soul and resurrection. Without these nothing persists to merit eternal life. It follows reasonably that the Christian belief in a post-mortem judgement of man's ethical worthiness that might merit eternal life could not have been derived from Greek, Hebrew, or Babylonian sources, none of which affirmed a concept of the individual soul's immortality or its resurrection. As the writer of Ecclesiastes put it, "All go unto one place; all are of dust, and all turn to dust again." (47) Nor can apocalyptic Judaism have provided the idea to early Christians. The Christian judgement applies to individuals, not an entire people or nation as in the apocalyptic view. Final judgement is rendered to all men, not just the members of the nation. As with so many other fundamental tenets of Christianity, there is no other source for Christianity's belief in a post-mortem judgement and eternal life but the traditional religion of Egypt.

Brandon points out that the idea of an afterlife can be found in Egypt as early as 3500 B.C.E.. By 2800 B.C.E. it had become closely connected with the notion that the *individual* could merit eternal life by living a morally worthy life on this earth. (48) To be sure proper ritual requirements had to be observed. But the idea that humans could earn life everlasting is among the oldest, most remarkable, and most impressive theological innovations in the history of man. That it was an Egyptian innovation is beyond doubt, for it is not found in any other theological system of the ancient West or Near East until it reappears within early Christianity. It is precisely the idea of eternal life that possessed the power to console, the reason to hope, the gospel or good news, that was at the center of Christianity's attractiveness just as it had been the attraction for Egyptians for the previous three thousand years. In both creeds the need to live a life of moral worthiness upon which a favorable judgement might be rendered did much to stimulate the casuistic development of ethical thinking.

Unlike the Egyptians, however, the Christians felt compelled to punish those upon whom an unfavorable judgement had been rendered after death and adopted the notion that these sinners went to a place of fiery torment. This vision of Hell seems to have come directly out of Jewish apocalyptic literature, most likely from the book of *Ezra* or *Enoch*. (49) By inventing a place of *eternal* torment Christians stood the concept of eternal reward on its head. If, as theologians were to argue later, man could not truly merit eternal life, then it is difficult to see how his sins could merit eternal damnation either. Egyptians, of course, settled the issue by holding that those judged not to be "true of voice" suffered "the Second Dying" and ceased to exist. To Christianity's credit, however, the promise of eternal life was not bound by race, nationality, or ethnicity. Among Christianity's great achievements was its extension of the promise, first made by Egypt's universal god, that salvation was offered to all men.

In attempting to hear the echoes of Egyptian religion across the millennia I have examined the theologies of the Osiran and Christian faiths to determine which, if any, Egyptian beliefs made their way into early Christian thinking and, if so, how this might have come about. The argument offered is that the principles of the Osiran faith were readily available and easily understood during the Ptolemaic period and Jesus' lifetime, having survived intact after three millennia of Egyptian theological and historical development. For three centuries before, and continuing until the end of Jesus' life and beyond, the Osiran faith underwent a strong and powerful revival that made it the official state religion of Ptolemaic Hellenism and the most widely-worshipped religion in the Mediterranean world until Theodosius put a violent end to paganism in 380 C.E. These powerful impulses were felt within the Palestine of Jesus' lifetime, even more strongly in Galilee because of its geographic location and demographic characteristics already mentioned. These factors and others strongly support the supposition that it is unlikely that Christ and his early followers could have remained ignorant of the beliefs and rituals of the commonly-present practice of the Osiris-Isis cult. The argument suggests that the linkage between Egyptian religion and Christianity, as an historical event occurring in time, cannot be reasonably rejected.

If it is likely that Egyptian religion was the historical source of early Christian beliefs, then the fundamental theological principles of both religions ought to be very similar and, if the direction of influence is correct, the similarities between Christian and Egyptian religions must be shown not to have been due to other sources, cultural or religious, extant at the time. The analysis presented here has compared each of the fundamental principles of early Christianity with the relevant principles found in the Egyptian, Babylonian, and Judaic religious traditions and in Greek Hellenism. In every case fundamental Christian principles were either not found in the other religions and philosophy or were found in a form that was radically different from those principles as understood by early Christians.

When compared with Egyptian sources, however, the following Christian beliefs were found to exist within the Osiris-Isis theology not only in identical *conceptual* form but also in the manner in which they were theologically *applied*. The conclusion offered here is that the Christian principles of (1) an incarnate god; (2) a god-head expressed in trinitarian form; (3) the individual's possession of an immortal soul; (4) resurrection; (5) a post-mortem judgement and (6) the promise of a reward of eternal life were adopted by early Christians from the original source, that is from the traditional theological doctrines of Egyptian religion that had existed for more than three thousand years before Jesus lived and which were widely held by the Osiran-Isis faith in Palestine and throughout the Roman world during his lifetime.

NOTES

1. John Dominic Crossan, *The Historical Jesus: The Life of a Mediterranean Jewish Peasant*, (San Francisco: Harper Collins, 1992), xxvii

2. Ibid., xxviii.

3. Hyam Maccoby, *The Mythmaker: Paul and the Invention of Christianity* (New York: Barnes and Noble, 1998), 12.

4. Ibid.

5. Peters, 498; see also B.R. Rees, "Popular Religion in Graeco-Roman Egypt: The Transition to Christianity," *Journal of Egyptian Archaeology*, vol. 36 (1950), 86-92.

6. Peters, 498.

7. Rees, 88.

8. Peters, 499.

9. Armstrong, 130.

10. E.A. Wallis Budge, *From Fetish to God in Ancient Egypt* (New York: Dover Publications, 1988), vi.

11. Morenz, 164.

12. *John* 1:1-3.

13. Morenz, 154.

14. Apparently the idea that god could be incarnate in images was not that far-fetched to early Christians. The *Apocryphal Gospels* tell of Mary and Jesus' arrival in Egypt. "There was a movement and quaking throughout the land and all the idols fell down from their pedestals and were broken in pieces. When the nobles went to a powerful priest who could speak with the devils in the idols for an explanation, he told them that the footsteps of the son "of the secret and hidden god" had fallen upon the land of Egypt." E.A. Wallis Budge, *Egyptian Magic* (New York: Dover Publications, 1971), 66.

15. Armstrong, 130.

16. Michael Grant, *Jesus: An Historian's View of the Gospels*, 117.

17. Ibid.

18. See Chapter 3 of this work.

19. S.G.F. Brandon, *Religion in Ancient History* (New York: Charles Scribner's Son, 1969), 344-347.

20. Morenz, 142.

21. H. Te Velde, "Some Remarks on the Structure of Egyptian Divine Triads," *Journal of Egyptian Archaeology*, vol. 57 (1971), 81.

22. Ibid.

23. Brandon, 83.

24. Ibid., 73.

25. Ibid., 79-80.

26. Ibid., 80.

27. Ibid.

28. Ibid., 73-74.

29. *Odyssey*, XI: 204-222.

30. Armstrong, 35.

31. Ibid., 36.

32. Ibid., 35.

33. Paul, 1 *Corinthians*, 15: 3-5.

34. Morton Smith, *Jesus the Magician* (New York: Barnes and Noble, 1993), 17.

35. Brandon, 82.

36. Rees, 93.

37. Smith, 17.

38. Peters, 326; see also Brandon, 113.

39. Michael Grant, *The Jews in the Roman World*, 37.

40. *Daniel* 12:2.

41. Crossan, 284.

42. Brandon, 114.

43. Tarn, 227.

44. Michael Grant, *The Jews in the Roman World*, 294.

45. Crossan, 388.

46. Brandon, 115.

47. *Ecclesiastes* 3:19.

48. Brandon, 112.

49. Peters, 326.

5

The Psychology Of Jesus The Egyptian

The thrust of the argument to this point is that Christianity derives the major premises of its theology from the Egyptian religious tradition, specifically the Osiris-Isis beliefs, that predated Christianity by several millennia. The protestations of some theologians to the contrary, Christianity did *not* derive from the Judaism of its day for the most basic of reasons: that both the theological premises of Judaism and many of its ritual practices stand in stark contradiction to those of Christianity. Judaism then and now affirmed the existence of a single god, but not one of a trinitarian nature; Judaism does not affirm the existence of an eternal soul, nor the possibility of resurrection, a final judgement beyond the grave, or eternal life, propositions fundamental to Christianity but absent in Judaism. The theological claim that Christianity derived from Judaism has no basis in historical fact or event. The only other possible source of the Christian theology is the Egyptian tradition. When I refer to Jesus as an Egyptian the intention is to draw attention to the fact that Jesus' theology and ritual practices are drawn from Egyptian tradition, and not to suggest that he was other than an Israelite.

The Temple authorities who confronted Jesus's claims could hardly have been unaware of the contradictions between the two faiths and challenged Jesus precisely on theological grounds, that is, that he was preaching blasphemy. Both Pilate and Herod seemed to have recognized this when they judged Jesus to have been innocent of any civil offense and returned him to the mercies of the religious police of the Jerusalem Temple. The Temple authorities also recognized that Christianity was a threat to Jewish doctrinal orthodoxy insofar as its premises stood in stark contradiction to Judaism's own teachings. It seems clear as well that they recognized the Egyptian origins of Jesus's teachings because they had been struggling for more than two centuries against the corrosive influence of the

105

Serapis-Isis cult whose beliefs must have seemed to the Temple authorities to be indistinguishable from those of Jesus himself. The similarity was not only evident in the doctrinal premises of Jesus' teachings, but in his adoption of ritual practices that were also Egyptian in origin and contrary to Jewish ritual law. Before Jesus, the threat to Jewish orthodoxy had come from without, from the Hellenistic Greeks who practiced the Osiran-Isis faith. Jesus represented a threat from within, a Jew who preached the pagan faith of the Egyptians and Greeks to his own people. For that reason Jesus had to be condemned.

Having examined the source of Jesus's theological teaching, we now turn to an examination of Jesus' rituals to determine if they also have their roots in Egyptian magical and ritual practice. Religious belief as intellectual adherence to a set of theological propositions said to "make sense" is most characteristic of theologians and not lay believers. For most people religious faith involves much more than intellectual assent and includes belief and participation in ritual and magic. This is even more the case in the formative period of any new religion. Over time all religions add rituals and magic to their repertoires so that rite and belief come to reenforce one another and in some cases become indistinguishable. Ritual and magic become equal in importance in affirming the religion's core beliefs in the eyes of the devout beholder. Sometimes continued adherence to a new faith depends more upon its rituals and magic than upon its intellectual appeal.

To the modern ear the word *magic* when used in a religious context might seem offensive. I do not mean it to be. I agree with John Crossan that there is nothing inherently pejorative in describing certain religious practices as magical. Religions themselves affirm that god is present during their services and employ ritual prayers to call upon him to do things for the assembled congregation. When practiced by a religious institution magic aims at making divine power present *indirectly through communal ritual*. When the same objective is sought by an *individual*, that is the magician, the god's presence is achieved *directly through personal miracle*. (1) Magic is essentially more a question of means rather than ends.

In his study of religious magic David Aune observes that magic and religion are so closely intertwined that it is virtually impossible to regard them as discrete socio-cultural categories. One man's magic is another's act of faith. Magic is a phenomenon that exists within the matrix of most religions and has a part to play that is defined by the religions institutions, beliefs, and values. To ask for the help of angels is good magic while calling upon demons is bad magic. It is the *context of magic*, i.e., its practice within acceptable institutional boundaries and values, rather than *magic per se* that assigns it a positive or negative quality. Magic appears to be "as universal a feature of religion as deviant behavior is of human societies." (2) All religions are possessed of magical rites, and rituals whose practice and exposition reenforce the believer's faith in its theological premises. To inquire into the sources of ritual and magic need not imply anything pejorative.

When religions are new they rely heavily upon ritual as a means of separating themselves from other creeds, especially so if the religion is a prosteletizing one and seeks to attract adherents from other creeds. The affirmation of the new through repudiation of the old occurs commonly throughout cultural history and is known as "normative inversion." (3) One way to prevent a new cult from being swallowed by the dominant culture is to affirm that those things that are abhorrent to the dominant culture are sacred to the new cult. This establishes the new cult's identity and uniqueness while making it impossible for the cult's members to return to the former creed. Moses did exactly that when he asked pharaoh for permission to take the Israelites into the desert for three days to make the spring sacrifice to Yahweh. Pharaoh asks why not hold your sacrifice in Egypt? Moses replies, *"Lo, if we shall sacrifice the abomination of the Egyptians, will they not stone us?"* (4) The Israelites intended to sacrifice the ram, a sacred animal and the very incarnation of the Egyptians' highest god, Amun. Nothing could have been more calculated to separate the Israelites from the Egyptians than this act of ritual deicide, an act that also established their respective religions as absolutely irreconcilable.

So it must have appeared to the Temple authorities when they learned that Jesus was affirming a trinitarian god. To orthodox Judaism this was akin to idolatry, and idolatry was among the worst ritual offenses that a Jew could commit. To the mind of the Sadducee idolatry meant the worship of the corpse of the Egyptian Osiris. A.S. Yahuda makes a strong case that the Israelites were acutely aware of the Osiris cult and railed against it vehemently although without using the name of Osiris. Throughout the Old Testament there are many references to idolaters which are referred to as *gillulim* in Hebrew. The word is taken from the Hebrew root *galol*, which means to wrap up or roll up. Yahuda suggests that the reference is to the Egyptian embalmed corpse, the *wt* in Egyptian or the "enwrapped one." (5) The god of the Jews was a living god and death was his principal taboo. Everything connected with death, especially the idols of the "enwrapped ones," but including mourning rituals, corpses, embalming, funerals, graveyards, and so on, was loathed. Who, then, would be more logically hated than Osiris, the Egyptian god of the dead, who was always portrayed as an "enwrapped one," a mummified corpse? (6) When the Israelites used the word *gillulim* to warn against idols, the reference was to Osiris. When Jesus seemed to be calling for the worship of the *gillulim* within the trinitarian god, to the Temple authorities he was calling for no less than the worship of the Egyptian god Osiris. One can hardly imagine a more inflammatory example of normative inversion.

Two ancient magical ritual traditions are relevant to this analysis: the Judaic tradition extant during the time of Jesus and the much older Egyptian Osiris-Isis theology that was thriving at the same time. The Judaic tradition had been strongly influenced by the Egyptian tradition until the time of the Babylonian exile (5th Century B.C.E.), at which time Judaism became heavily influenced by Babylonian ritual magic. The ritual influences of the East—astrology, demonology, ritualistic conjuring, etc.—were felt within the Judaic tradition, and Jewish magicians came to be held in high esteem. (7) In both Greek and Egyptian magical papyri of the time Yahweh is mentioned repeatedly for his usefulness in magic. In these pagan documents it is noteworthy that the name of Yahweh as a magical charm outnumbers the name of any other deity by three to one. (8) By the end of the first century Jewish magicians had codified their magic in the *Sefer ha-Razim* (the Book of Secrets), a magical text that gave directions for manipulating demonic powers by prayer and sacrifices. (9) It was out of a branch of this Jewish-Babylonian magical tradition that Jesus emerged.

The northern (Samarian/Galileean) Jewish magical tradition from which Christ came was different from the southern (Judean) tradition. In the south prophets and magicians were honored for their words and deeds as instruments of god. The northern tradition was much more radical, and constituted a special brand of prophetic tradition going back to Elijah and Elisha in which oracular political prophecy and individual magic manifested through spells and miracle cures were central. (10) Within this tradition the magicians and holy men were revered not just for their words and deeds, but for their claim to possess a personal relationship with god that transcended the usual priestly structure and ritual of the community. These magicians combined prophecy with magic and became magical prophets. (11) They summoned god directly through personal miracle by-passing or even rejecting the usual means of summoning god indirectly through communal ritual. In the northern Jewish tradition the magical prophet was a type of wonder-worker who operated with certain divine authority neither mediated by nor dependent upon the usual forms, rituals, and institutions (the priesthood and temple sacrifice) through which divine power was usually seen to operate. (12) Under these circumstances conflict between the magical prophets and the established religion was inevitable.

Jewish magicians were usually men of the people and walked among them. This gave them a very different perspective on the world from the elite priesthood who opposed them, and often included terrible visions of destruction for a social order they regarded as unjust. They wandered from place to place preaching this peasant apocalyptism, performing miracles and administering cures to common people. The Gospels record examples of Jesus' magic during his wanderings noting that he performed six exorcisms, seventeen healings, and eight nature miracles. Some of these magicians went further and claimed that they could forgive sins by touching or incantation becoming a threat to the religious establishment which claimed that only temple sacrifice could successfully beseech god to forgive sins. (13)

It is likely that these magical prophets were more common than the surviving historical records suggest. Within the first seventy years of the First century of the Common Era, including Jesus' lifetime, history has left us as examples of the prophet magicians of northern Israel the names of Ben-Dosa, Jesus himself, Judas the Galileean, Simon of Perea, Anthronges of Judea, and a very curious fellow known only as "the Egyptian" who gathered several thousand followers at the Mount of Olives in expectation of the Messiah's arrival before being arrested by the Romans. His ultimate fate is unknown.

The Judaic magical tradition was comprised of two main streams, the Babylonian and the Egyptian. The Egyptian influence was the more profound cultural influence on Judaism right from the beginning, and even though the Babylonian influence was very strong during the Ptolemaic and early Roman periods, it by no means completely eclipsed the Egyptian influence. While it is likely that some Egyptian magical practices had been associated with Judaism for a long time, it was only after the return from exile in Babylon that these practices were officially codified within Judaism itself. Other practices current in Egyptian magic at that time were probably included as well. It is likely, then, that the Jewish magical tradition contains within it both very old and comparatively recent (5th-4th Century B.C.E.) borrowings from the Egyptian magical tradition. For example, the use of the *tefilin* as representative of the pharaonic *ureaus* probably dates from the days of Akhenaten, while the design of the Ark of the Covenant as described by Ezekiel may only date from the period immediately after the return from Babylon. Like the Osiran-Isis theological tradition the Egyptian magical tradition persisted in an unbroken line from time immemorial until it was liquidated by the Christian emperors in the Fourth century C.E. The Egyptian magical tradition was a profound influence upon both the Judaic and Christian magical traditions.

The Egyptian magician was a very influential figure. The great magicians were recognized by Pharaoh himself as the official directors of religious and magical ceremonies and were given the title of *Kher heb*. (14) Egyptian magicians were widely regarded as important men even in Israel. Egyptian magical amulets are among the most common archaeological finds in Israel today. (15) The Egyptian magician recited spells, incantations, prayers and other magical formulae often with terrifying effects. Greek writers of the period record that Egyptian sorcerers could send horrifying dreams to men and women to steal their minds and senses. Such magicians could cause lust in a person, or sickness, and even death. Raising the dead was said to be a common occurrence, as was the ability of Egyptian magicians to assume animal forms or make themselves invisible. (16) Other texts tell of Egyptian magicians' ability to foretell the future, explain auguries and portents, interpret dreams, diagnose illnesses, declare the names of the spirits of the dead, concoct potions and medicines, and recite the secret names of the gods. (17)

The influence of Egyptian magic upon Christianity was evident early when Christian "holy men" performed some of the same magical feats in the name of Jesus as Egyptian magicians. Early texts note that Macarius changed a woman who had been turned into a mare back again by sprinkling holy water upon her. Paul the Simple, an early monk, was said to have cast out a devil that had taken the form of a "mighty dragon 70 cubits long." Another monk, Po Apollo, cast a spell upon a group of people worshipping a pagan image immobilizing them so they could not escape the heat of the blazing sun. One Petarpemotis was said to have made a dead man speak. (18)

Because an Egyptian magical tradition existed alongside Christianity during its formative period, the question arises whether any Egyptian magical rituals and practices can be found within Christianity to confirm the influence of Egyptian magic upon Christian practice? Not surprisingly one does not have to look very far to discover examples of Egyptian magic within the rites and rituals of Jesus' Christianity. To the orthodox Jewish religious establishment the charge of Egyptian magic would have been a powerful counterargument to the claim of Jesus's followers that he was the son of god.

Charges of magical practice within Christianity arose almost immediately after Jesus's death as his enemies sought to discredit his life and teaching. One of the more common accusations was that Jesus had spent time in Egypt where he gained knowledge of Egyptian magical practices. The attempt to discredit this accusation, Morton Smith argues, explains why the story of Jesus' flight to Egypt occurs only in the gospel of Matthew. Matthew has Joseph and Mary fleeing to Egypt shortly after Jesus's birth to avoid Herod's wrath over the rumor that a new king had been born among the people. Like any good propagandist Matthew sets out to discredit the charge by admitting to part of it while discounting its substance. Matthew admits that Jesus had gone to Egypt, but had done so as an infant and therefore the charge that he had learned Egyptian magic there was untrue. (19)

Despite Jesus' followers' attempts to discredit the accusation that he practiced Egyptian magic, the charge never really disappeared. Matthew's story about Jesus' Egyptian sojourn remains for some scholars unconvincing, as it must have for those critics of Jesus' day. The Gospels are silent about the first twelve years of Jesus' life. There is no mention of Jesus' practice of Judaism at all in three of the gospels. Only Luke *hints* at Jesus' observance of Judaism when he tells us that he was circumcised (*Luke* 2:21), that his parents took him to the Jerusalem temple when his mother was purified in a ritual in which doves were sacrificed (*Luke* 2:22), and that his parents were observant, traveling to Jerusalem every year for the ritual of Passover (*Luke* 2:41) After his birth we do not encounter Jesus again until he is found, as Luke says, "teaching in the synagogue" at twelve years of age.

In the modern era we are used to thinking of a twelve year old as still very much of a child. But in antiquity a twelve year old was already an adult. It was the age at which a boy was permitted full participation in Jewish religious rituals. In Egypt the average age of marriage in the New Kingdom was between twelve and thirteen, and Egyptian women usually gave birth to their first child by fourteen. A youth of twelve would have already completed his formal education in an Egyptian House of Life where he learned to read and write and studied the arts of his trade or profession. In the process, of course, an Egyptian youth would have become thoroughly familiar with the principles and beliefs of the Egyptian Osiris-Isis religion. If we combine Matthew's account that Jesus was taken by his parents to Egypt with his absence of twelve years, we might reasonably surmise that Jesus remained in Egypt for that time where he might have been exposed to Egyptian magic as a matter of course.

The virtue of Christ's hidden years for researchers is that they may be filled with any number of explanations. It is interesting nonetheless to speculate about what Jesus' time in Egypt might have been like. When Joseph and Mary left Israel for Egypt, as Matthew says they did, they would most likely have sought out relatives, if they had any, at one of the many Jewish communities that had been established in Egypt during the Ptolemaic period. These communities were most often located in cities or large towns. Here Joseph might have found employment and Jesus would have found the opportunity for an education. Any Egyptian town of any size had a temple to Osiris-Isis to which would likely have been attached a House of Life, a scriptorum where Egyptians educated their children. It would not have been unusual for the town to have a Greek *gymnasium*, a primary-high school equivalent where Greeks educated their young. By Jesus' time the *gymnasium* had been heavily Egyptianized in terms of curriculum and rituals. Greeks matriculating from the *gymnasium* in Egypt often swore their oaths to Egyptian gods. If, as some assert, Jesus was literate and spoke Greek, he could have learned these skills at the *gymnasium* while a boy in Egypt.

To remain in Egypt for some time might have appeared attractive to Joseph and Mary for other reasons. The rumors of infidelity that surrounded Mary's pregnancy were absent in Egypt and presented no barrier to the advancement of their son, as they might have in Israel. In Egypt Jesus would have had the opportunity for an education. In Israel Jesus' questionable lineage might have made it difficult for him to receive even a rudimentary synagogue education which, in any case, would have consisted of little more than learning to read Jewish religious texts. Egypt offered much greater opportunities. In either the House of Life or the *gymnasium* the boy could study subjects—medicine, the trades, law—not available to him in Israel while becoming literate in Greek and Egyptian. Judging from the intellectual activity of the Jewish community in Alexandria, Jews apparently were able to avail themselves of both Greek and Egyptian educational opportunities with little difficulty. Had Joseph and Mary remained in Egypt for Jesus' twelve "hidden years" it might well have been to provide themselves and their son with a better life than they would have had in a small town in Israel. Almost a million Jews had already settled in Egypt during the Ptolemaic period. Another Jewish family living in Egypt at the time would have been unremarkable.

Spending his youth in Egypt would have provided Jesus with plenty of opportunity to become familiar with Egyptian magic. Magic was such a fundamental part of Egyptian life, and magicians, soothsayers, and sorcerers so common, that it would have been remarkable if Jesus was able to remain unaware of their activities. Apart from this, is there any evidence of Egyptian magic in Jesus' personal behavior and religious rites? As Morton Smith has argued in his fascinating work, *Jesus the Magician*, the circumstantial evidence is strong that Jesus was familiar with Egyptian magic and practiced it. Among the more interesting evidence is the possibility that Jesus himself may have carried the tatoo marks of the Egyptian magician. Tattooing charms, sacred signs, prayers, and spells upon one's flesh was a common practice for all magicians, including Egyptian magicians. Directions for doing so are given plainly in the *Greek Magical Papyri* and other magical texts of the period. (20) The evidence for Jesus having magical tattoos comes from both Jewish and Christian sources.

The rabbinic tradition of stories about Jesus begins about the same time that Josephus wrote *Antiquities* during the last half of the First century of the Common Era. One of these stories recounts the arrest of a distinguished rabbi named Eliezer (70-100 C.E.?) who as an old man was arrested by Jewish authorities on the suspicion that he was secretly a Christian. (21) During the trial Eliezer enters into a discussion with another rabbi over whether or not a man who cuts tatoos or letters in his flesh on the Sabbath is in violation of sabbath law. The other rabbis argue that the man is innocent. Eliezer argues for his guilt in effect saying that in other cases people who did this were found to be guilty. Eliezer says, "But is it not [the case that] Ben Stada (Jesus) brought magic marks from Egypt in the scratches on his flesh?" The other rabbi replied. "He was a madman and you cannot base laws on [the actions of] madmen." (22) One infers from this ancient transcript that magical tatoos were a well-known phenomenon; that it was commonly believed among the rabbis that Jesus was himself tattooed in the manner of Egyptian magicians; and that Jesus obtained these tatoos in Egypt before returning to Israel. (23)

Smith argues that the Eliezer record is very important and probably accurate. The story does not, as with some other accounts, appear in the polemical literature, but seems to be a straight-forward account of a legal proceeding. Eliezer tells the story as part of the larger case at issue. It is offered as a passing reference to prove only a minor point. It is clear, however, that the other rabbis knew immediately who Jesus was, believed that he was tattooed, and that he had obtained these tatoos in Egypt. Smith concludes that "the antiquity of the source, type of citation, connection with the report that he was in Egypt, and agreement with Egyptian magical practices, are considerable arguments in its favor." (24)

The charge that Jesus was tattooed with magical marks receives additional support from Christian sources, most pointedly from Saint Paul. In *Galatians* 6:17 Paul seems to be claiming that he bears special marks on his body similar to those carried by Jesus. Paul says, *"From now on, let no one make troubles for me; for I bear the marks of Jesus on my body."* This statement has puzzled Christian scholars for a long time who, Macoby says, have resolved the dilemma by suggesting that Paul was claiming to possess the stigmata of Jesus. (25) But there is no evidence anywhere in any source that points to an awareness on the part of anyone that the stigmata were known during the time of early Christianity. The first recorded instance of the stigmata occurred during the Middle Ages when Francis of Assisi (1182-1226 C.E.) was said to have manifested the wounds of Jesus upon his body. (26) The onset of stigmata during Paul's day would have astounded both Christian and pagan alike, and would almost certainly have resulted in some record of its occurrence somewhere.

If not the stigmata, then to what could Paul have been referring when he claimed to bear the "marks of Jesus" upon his flesh? One possibility favored by some biblical historians is that Paul is referring to the scars he received from beatings and stonings that he endured during his apostolic work. Another is that Paul wore the brand of the slave. It was not uncommon for slaves to be branded or tattooed to show to whom they belonged. But there is no evidence that Paul had ever been a slave or, indeed, that Jesus bore a slave mark. Another possibility is that Paul bore a mark indicating a previous allegiance to some pagan god. In commentary upon Paul's claim *The New American Bible* notes that devotees of pagan gods sometimes had marks of identification burned into their flesh. (27) Paul came from the city of Tarsus where there was a temple to the pagan god Attis. Given Paul's propensity to change religions and to embrace each with equal fervor, it is not impossible that he may have been a follower of the Attis cult. But as far as we know the cult did not require tattooing. Some of the cult members venerated their god by castrating themselves, but this is a far cry from tattooing. (28)

Even if Paul did bear the mark of Attis, it strains credulity that he would have been able to pass it off as a mark also possessed by Jesus. It is possible Paul was claiming to have the same "scratches" or tatoos that the rabbinic tradition claims Jesus possessed. The point is that in mounting his own claim Paul seems to be confirming that Jesus did indeed possess some marks or tattoos of which others were aware as the rabbinic tradition affirms. If Jesus did not possess them and they were fabrications of Jesus' enemies, then why did Paul claim to possess them at all? One reasonable conclusion is simply that Jesus did in fact bear the tattoos of the Egyptian magician, tattoos which the rabbinical tradition says he acquired as a young man in Egypt.

The Eucharistic sacrifice is the most magic-soaked ritual of Christianity and is most likely of Egyptian origin, although elements of it can be found in other pagan rituals. The central idea of the Eucharistic sacrifice is that Jesus transformed bread and wine at his last supper with his apostles into his own body and blood which was then consumed by the apostles as a way of uniting them with Jesus. All four writers of the Gospels present some version of this story. Matthew tells us that *"while they were eating, Jesus took bread, said the blessing, broke it, and giving it to his disciples said, "Take and eat; this is my body." Then he took a cup, gave thanks, and gave it to them, saying, "Drink from it, all of you, for this is my blood of the covenant, which will be shed on behalf of many for the forgiveness of sins."* (29)

The idea of transforming bread and wine by magic into the magician's body and blood so that the food becomes endowed with magical powers and then sharing it with another person who by eating it becomes united with the magician is an old ritual and one that was routinely practiced by Egyptian magicians of the day. (30) Whoever eats of the magical food becomes united in and identified with the magician. If, as in some cults, the magician is thought to be a god, then the subject is united with the god as well. Jesus's magic ritual was designed to bond his apostles to him in the same manner any Egyptian magician might use the ritual for the same purpose.

The sense of magic in Jesus' use of this ritual is appreciated if we remember that the Last Supper was not the only occasion where Jesus is said to have used it. He employed it again in other contexts suggesting that consuming flesh and blood as votive food was a commonly known magical rite, as indeed it was among pagan magicians. John records that at the occasion of the multiplication of the loaves at Capernaum Jesus said, *"I am the living bread that come down from heaven; whoever eats this bread will live forever; and the bread that I will give is my flesh for the life of the world."* (31) The message is clear that all who eat the magic foods will be bound for eternity to the magician-god. Jesus goes on to say, *"Whoever eats my flesh and drinks my blood has eternal life, and I will raise him on the last day. For my flesh is true food, and my blood is true drink. Whoever eats my flesh and drinks my blood remains in me and I in him."* (my emphasis) (32)

Thus it is that the god comes to dwell in the subject through magic, and the subject comes to dwell in the god. It is difficult to avoid the impression that this is a magical application of the Egyptian doctrine of incarnation in which the gods come to dwell in things, in this case individuals who partake of the ritual. The Eucharistic rite understood as transformation of body and blood was sufficiently common and known to be used in contexts beyond the idea of a special singular occurrence at the Last Supper. In this regard it is like all other magic.

Morton Smith suggests that accounts of the Eucharistic ritual found in surviving magical texts "have their closest parallels in Egyptian texts." (33) Smith draws upon the material contained in the *Demotic Magical Papyrus* for examples of eucharistic rites that are similar to the text of the institution of the Christian eucharist. (34) The *Demotic Magical Papyrus* was written in the third century C.E., but its contents are much older. The first writing of the text cited here was most probably around the time of Jesus. Written in both demotic and hieratic, the text is a collection of spells and invocations and contains examples of rituals using vessels and various fluids including animal blood. Smith offers the example of one such Egyptian ritual. The magician mingles various ingredients in a cup of wine and pronounces the following words over it.

> *"I am he of Abydos...I am this figure of one drowned that testifieth by writing*
>
> *...as to which the blood of Osiris bore witness...when it was poured in this*
>
> *cup, this wine. Give it, blood of Osiris that he gave to his Isis to make her*
>
> *feel love in her heart for him...give it, the blood of (magician's name) to...(recipient's*
>
> *name) in this cup, this bowl of wine, today, to cause her to feel a love for him*
>
> *in her heart, the love that Isis felt for Osiris..."* (35)

The ritual seems designed to cause a woman to feel love for a man. What is important is that the magical methodology is identical to the eucharistic ritual in which the magician-god gives his own body and blood to a recipient who, by eating or drinking it, will be united with the magician in some way. The ritual is surely Egyptian in practice if not in origin (which is lost in any case) and if Jesus knew Egyptian magic, would have been as familiar to him as to any other Egyptian magician.

John's Gospel notes that the eucharist ritual caused great concern among the Jews who heard Jesus preach at Capernaum. Hearing Jesus offer his body and blood, John records them saying, *"How can this man give us his flesh to eat?."* (36) They might well have thought Jesus mad. Christian theologians have made much of the claim that the eucharist pronounced at the Last Supper has its roots in the Jewish passover meal. But by no stretch of the theological imagination can the eucharist be regarded as having its roots in any Jewish religious practice. First, the notion of drinking blood—symbolic or otherwise—is anathema to Jews and has been since the time of Moses. It is among the most ancient Judaic taboos. The very idea of touching, to say nothing of drinking, blood was a ritual atrocity. This element of the eucharistic rite is completely non-Jewish in origin and practice, and by no reasonable argument can it be made an extension of Jewish ritual practice. As Morton Smith so candidly puts it, "To try to derive them (the Eucharistic rituals) from the passover ritual or any other Jewish rite is ludicrous. Strange as some rituals of Judaism might be, they do not include eating people." (37)

Nor can the *central idea* of the eucharist be reasonably derived from Judaic religious practice. The notion that by eating the body and blood of the god one can become one with the godhead who is divine and died for our sins is so obviously Osiran as to be beyond reasonable question. The idea of a blood sacrifice of a human was anathema to the Jews for it amounts to a reinstatement of human sacrifice which the Jews had long since abandoned and which was forbidden by Jewish law. (38) The two central elements of the Christian eucharistic rite are clearly of pagan origin, mostly likely Egyptian, and would have been well-known to any Egyptian magician of the time.

Another Egyptian ritual practiced by Jesus was baptism. Baptism is the most fundamental Christian rite insofar as one must be baptized to become a full participant in the rituals of the Christian faith. Over the centuries baptism came to represent both the initiation of the person into the Christian faith and the forgiveness of sin. With the introduction of infant baptism in the modern period, the emphasis was placed upon being brought into the faith rather than upon the forgiveness of sin, although Christians maintain that baptism removes the "original sin" of the infant. Its use by John the Baptist, however, was the reverse. John used baptism as a ritual means of forgiving sins. In antiquity sickness and sin were often equated with illness being seen as divine punishment for the sinner's transgressions.

When the Baptist (and later Jesus) cured people by ritual and baptism, he was also forgiving sins. (39) This subverted the Judaic religious authorities who held a monopoly on the forgiveness of sin by requiring temple sacrifice to beseech god to forgive the sinner. It is only with Jesus' baptism that the ritual acquired the implication of an initiation rite, of being made fit to be brought into the presence of the religious community and of god; indeed, to have god enter and dwell within the person. Over the centuries the meaning of baptism as initiation superseded its importance as a means of forgiving sins. Sins were still "washed away," but the primary value of being "born again" was to be made fit to join the community of believers and permit god to "enter one's heart."

The origins of baptism are Egyptian, although it is not necessarily likely that John the Baptist, who seems to have introduced the rite to Christians, obtained it from this source. Crossan suggests that "archaic water-rituals of purification" were transformed by John into "a magic ritual that saves." (40) In explaining John's practice of baptism *The New American Bible* notes that various forms of ritual washing by various groups were common in Palestine between 150 B.C.E. and 250 C.E.. (41) John may have copied the water ritual from the purificatory washings of the Essenes in Qumran. (42) If we separate the ritual of baptism into its two elements—ritual washing to forgive sins and the transformation of the individual to receive god—then it is reasonable that John copied the ritual washing from elsewhere, for it was not a common Jewish practice. Through his baptism Jesus established the transformation element later. If, however, we regard the two elements as ritually inseparable, then the only place where both elements are found in a similar ritual is in Egypt, what Gardiner calls the rite of "baptism of pharaoh." (43)

The Egyptian baptismal rite has its origins in the Heliopolitan worship of the sun early in the Pyramid Age. The Egyptians believed that each morning the sun passed through the waters of the ocean before being reborn each day and emerging purified and revitalized. The ritual baptism of the pharaoh each morning symbolized this event and renewed the life and vigor of the recipient. (44) At the start of each day pharaoh entered the temple called the House of Morning where the king prepared to make himself worthy to greet the sun god. Two priests representing the gods Toth and Horus sprinkled him with water from the Sacred Lake of the temple. This holy water was believed to possess special properties for it was believed to be the body fluid of Osiris himself. (45) Although the ritual was of solar origin, by the time of the New Kingdom Osiran elements came to play a major role in it. The officiating priests, for example, wore the masks of Toth and Horus, both of which had prominent roles in the Osiran myth. It was these gods who performed the ritual of resurrection over the corpse of Osiris. New life was brought to Osiris' limbs and body by washing clearly linking washing with magic water to rebirth. (46)

As if to insure that observers understood that the king was being transformed and reborn, portrayals of pharaoh's baptism show a water jug held over his head with water pouring from it. The water is depicted not by the hieroglyph for water, but with the *ankh*, the hieroglyph that symbolizes life. (47) So important was the ritual of baptism to the Egyptians that some form of it became an essential rite in all important religious and state rituals. It even appeared in the funerary liturgy where the daily ritual was repeated in the washing of the dead.

Although baptism as ritual washing to cleanse oneself is a very old rite in Egyptian theology, it is important to understand that its origins and meaning *do not lie in the forgiveness of sin* as they seem to have for John the Baptist. Egyptian baptism was meant to prepare the recipient to enter into the presence of god or, as later when the Osiran doctrine of personal piety and sin moved to the forefront of Egyptian religion, to prepare the recipient to receive the god within him. Thus it was through baptism that one was "reborn" or made worthy of union with god.

Such an idea is not, of course, very different from the idea that baptism conferred a "state of grace" necessary to enter into the presence of the god. Gardiner recognized the similarity between the Egyptian and Christian rites. "The analogy of our rite (Egyptian) to that of Christian baptism is close enough....In both cases a symbolic cleansing by means of water serves as initiation into a properly legitimized religious life." (48) Gardiner suggests that the meaning and significance of this baptism is brought out by an inscription of a wall-scene in the great hall at Karnak. The scene portrays Sethos I being purified by the water of life. The accompanying words read, *"I purify thee with life and dominion, that thou mayest grow young, like thy father Re, and make a jubilee-festival like Atum, being arisen gloriously as prince of joy."* (49)

The Egyptian rite of baptism's emphasis upon transforming the recipient so that he is acceptable to god is almost identical in meaning to what Christians attribute to Jesus when he was baptized. Both rites are also quite different from John's use of baptism as a means to forgive sins. Even John seems to have recognized this. When Jesus came to be baptized, John tried to dissuade him, for Jesus had no sins to be forgiven. It was not merely an issue of which man was superior in stature in god's eyes. It was rather the relevance of baptism at all to a man who had never known sin. Jesus' baptism was *not* about forgiveness of sin but about *establishing his divinity* in the eyes of men and receiving the god-head within him. Matthew describes the event with the same drama as an Egyptian priest might describe the baptism of pharaoh. Matthew recounts, *"After Jesus was baptized, he came up from the water and behold, the heavens were opened for him, and he saw the Spirit of God descending like a dove and coming upon him. And a voice came from the heavens, saying, "This is my beloved Son, with whom I am well pleased."* (50)

In explaining this event *The New American Bible* asserts "The baptism of Jesus is the occasion on which he is equipped for his ministry by the Holy Spirit and proclaimed to be the son of god." (51) Through his baptism Christ is reborn in that like the Egyptian king his divinity is reaffirmed and his powers drawn from god are confirmed once again. Neither Jesus' baptism nor Egyptian baptism were about washing away sins or seeking forgiveness for them. Both were about divinities reaffirming their divinity through ritual and preparing themselves for the special tasks that divinity conferred upon both. Seen in this light, John the Baptist's puzzlement on the banks of the Jordan is understandable. As a wandering ascetic who saw visions, it is unlikely that John would have known about the rites of Egyptian baptism. If Jesus had knowledge of Egyptian religion and magic, then he would have known both its ritual and meaning. If he were seeking to lay claim to a special relationship with the god-head (Jesus called Him *Abba* or father) and to divine powers, Jesus could hardly have a chosen a more appropriate ritual than Egyptian baptism.

If forgiveness of sin was not an integral element of the original Egyptian ritual, how did John the Baptist come to use it as such? It is possible that, as Crossan suggests, he might have adopted it from the Essenes. That leaves open the question of its origin since Jews did not usually practice ritual washing for that purpose. Ritual washing in one form or another had probably been around in many cultures for millennia. But ritual washing *specifically to forgive sin* is quite another matter and requires some idea of sin that transcends purely ritual offenses; sin that includes unacceptable personal and social behavior for which the individual feels himself responsible.

It was the Egyptians who began to develop the idea of sin in conjunction with the evolution of social ethics and the democratization of the Osiran myth before the New Kingdom. The idea of personal responsibility for sin had to await the turning inward to personal piety and a personal relationship with god that developed after the 9th century B.C.E. By Ptolemaic times the idea of sin and personal responsibility for it had re-emerged full blown in conjunction with the Osiris-Isis religion and found a receptive audience among Greeks, Romans, and Jews. It was probably during this period that Egyptians began to regard ritual cleansing as a means of absolving oneself from sin even as the original significance of the washing was based in the ancient doctrine of reaffirming the solar-divinity of the king. (52) Once established in Ptolemaic Egypt, the idea of baptism as a means of forgiving sins might easily have made its way into Palestine where the Essenes, John the Baptist, and others might have adopted it. Even so, this would not account for baptism as a ritual understood by early Christians to transform them in a manner in which they could "live" in the god and the god "live" in them. It was a meaning that would have been incomprehensible to a Jew, Roman, Babylonian or Greek. But one that would have been instantly recognized by an Egyptian magician.

Much of what Jesus espoused as theology and practiced as ritual would have been obvious to any follower of the Osiris-Isis faith, although it appeared blasphemous to the Judaism of Jesus' day. If so, then there is no escaping the conclusion that Jesus' behavior involved "normative inversions." And deliberately so. Jesus' theological affirmations and his ritual practices could not have been more calculated to separate his followers from the theology and rituals of Judaism. Which raises the question of the *human motivation* behind Jesus' actions. Put another way, why would Jesus reject the premises and practices of his religion as clearly as he did? It is hardly likely that Jesus thought of himself as a Jewish reformer. There is no evidence in the Jesus saga that he was an observant Jew, and it is unlikely that anyone less than an observant Jew would have been interested in religious reform. Given that most of the population of Galilee during Jesus' day was pagan, it is just as likely that Jesus could have been a follower of the Isis cult to begin with! The gospels offer us no information regarding Jesus' practice of Judaism. Jesus' rejection of Judaism may have been a reaction to Judaism's rejection of him as a young man due, perhaps, to the persistent rumors of his illegitimacy.

That such rumors followed Jesus all his life seems clear enough from the Jesus saga itself. Matthew deals with the issue in the first chapter of his gospel, something we would not expect if the charge had not gained some degree of validity in the minds of his audience. *Matthew* tells us in 1:18-19 that, *"Now the birth of Jesus the Messiah took place in this way. When his mother Mary had been engaged to Joseph, but before they lived together, she was found to be with child from the Holy Spirit. Her husband, Joseph, being a righteous man and unwilling to expose her to public disgrace, planned to dismiss her quietly."* Here we encounter elements of the Isis myth. Isis, too, conceived the god Horus after her husband, Osiris, was dead leaving her open to the charge of infidelity and her son to the charge of illegitimacy. Even Joseph believed that Mary had been unfaithful, for he "planned to dismiss her quietly," that is, to divorce her, only to be talked out of it by an angel who convinced him that Mary was impregnated by the Holy Spirit. We may reasonably surmise that the people of Nazareth were less inclined to believe the tale, and probably came to regard Jesus as the illegitimate child of Mary.

In the normal course of things Jesus' illegitimacy would have presented no barriers to the young man, save the taunting that often accompanies such circumstances in a small town. Illegitimacy, by itself, would not have had any *religious* consequences for Jesus. Orthodox Judaism defines a Jew as a child of a Jewish mother, adopting the Egyptian matrilineal model. The child's paternity is of no *religious* consequence. But in Mary's case the charge was far more serious. Mary was charged with conceiving a child *by marital infidelity*, becoming pregnant by someone other than Joseph while she was betrothed to him. Marital infidelity was punishable by death by stoning. Mary's situation was a very different matter indeed from illegitimacy and involved grave religious implications. In Jewish tradition the child of an adulterous relationship is called a *mamzer* and is denied participation in Jewish religious rituals. In the tribal society of ancient Israel where blood lineage was the root of tribal membership, a *mamzer* was a social and religious outcast. Often hounded from their native villages, these outcasts wandered from village to town, forced to move whenever their stigma was discovered.

This fate might have befallen the young Jesus, and might account for the absence of any information in the Jesus saga about his religious life prior to his ministry. If he was known to be a *mamzer,* he would not have been permitted membership in the village congregation. Jesus' violent rejection by his neighbors in Nazareth may be explainable in similar terms. All of the Gospels record that when Jesus returned to Nazareth to preach, he did so on the sabbath and in a synagogue addressing the congregation. Matthew, Mark, and John tell us that the congregation "took offense at him." But Luke's account of the incident is more revealing and consistent with the reaction of a Jewish congregation to a *mamzer*. After noting that the people drew attention to Jesus' lineage—*"Is this not the carpenter, the son of Mary?"*—[there is no mention of Joseph]—the congregation grew angry and tried to kill Jesus! As *Luke* 4:28-30 tells it, *"When they heard this, all in the synagogue were filled with rage. They got up, drove him out of town, and led him to the brow of the hill on which their town was built, so that they might hurl him off the cliff. But he passed through the midst of them and went on his way."* [Tourist guides still point out the location of the cliff in Nazareth.] This was a serious incident. Jesus may well have "offended" other congregations, but none of them approached the violence of the congregation in Nazareth, the one place where we may be reasonably certain his questionable paternity was known.

Jesus' reputation as a *mamzer* may explain why he was unmarried and why, as the Jesus saga tells us, he chose to remain celibate as well. Celibacy for religious reasons was rare, but not unknown to the Jews of Jesus' time. Celibacy was practiced by the proto-monastic community at Qumran, probably by religious iconoclasts like John the Baptist and although we are not certain, probably among some ranks of the Egyptian Isis priesthood. But in Jewish society where lineage was extremely important and where male children were required to guarantee inheritance, marriage was the normal circumstance of the Jewish male. Being without a wife would have been regarded by the Jews of Jesus' day as an unfortunate condition resulting from being too poor to afford a wife, being afflicted by physical or mental illness, or the consequence of some reason of religious ritual that would have made the person religiously unacceptable.

The rumor that Jesus was the product of his mother's marital infidelity placed him beyond the Jewish religious community, and would certainly have made him an unattractive marriage prospect to any Jewish woman of even common standing. The Gospels make much of the fact that Jesus associated with women of low standing, among them an adulteress, a prostitute, and a women possessed by demons. Because of their circumstances all of these women were outcasts from their communities, and may have been the only women who were willing to associate with Jesus, who was himself an outcast.

If Jesus was aware of the rumors of his mother's infidelity, we would not be surprised if he came to harbor anger and resentment both toward her and his family. It was they, after all, who were responsible for his situation. From this perspective, the Gospel passages in which Jesus speaks disparagingly of his family appear more comprehensible. Again and again, Jesus appears to devalue the family. In *Matthew* 10: 34-36 he says, *"I have not come to bring peace, but a sword. For I have come to set a man against his father, and his daughter against her mother, and a daughter-in-law against her mother-in-law; and one's foes will be members of one's own household."* Mark records that when Mary and his family came to take him home because some of the townspeople had told them Jesus was insane or possessed, Jesus rejected them out of hand and refused to see them. When told his mother and family "were outside" calling for him, he replied, *"Who are my mother and my brothers?" And looking at those around him, he said, "Here are my mother and brothers!"* (*Mark* 3:33-35) In *Matthew* 10:37 Jesus says, *"Whoever loves father or mother more than me is not worthy of me; and whoever loves son or daughter more than me is not worthy of me."* Perhaps the strongest and most disturbing of Jesus' utterances rejecting family loyalties is recorded by *Luke* 14:25-26. *"Now large crowds were travelling with him; and he turned and said to them, "Whoever comes to me and does not hate his father and mother, wife and children, brothers and sisters, yes, and even life itself, cannot be my disciple."* That an illegitimate child might come to focus his resentment upon the people responsible for his circumstances is hardly surprising.

The Jesus saga reveals several instances where Jesus rejects his mother by treating her badly in front of others. At Cana, for example, *John* 2:5 tells us that *"There was a wedding at Cana of Galilee and Jesus' mother was there. When the wine gave out, Mary approached Jesus and said, "They have no wine." And Jesus said to her, "Woman, what concern is that to you and to me? My hour has not yet come." His mother told the servants, "Do whatever he tells you."* The gospels record only two instances when Jesus addressed his mother directly. The first was at Cana and the second, recorded only by John, was at the crucifixion itself. *John* 19:26-27 records the event thus. *"When Jesus saw his mother and the disciple whom he loved standing beside her, he said to his mother, "Woman, here is your son." Then he said to his disciple, "Here is your mother." And from that hour the disciple [unnamed] took her into his own home."* Nowhere in the gospels, not even on the eve of his own death, does Jesus ever refer to his mother as mother.

It is also intriguing that Jesus addresses the issue of divorce in terms that seem to refer to his mother's marital infidelity. In *Matthew* 5:32 Jesus says, *"But I say to you that anyone who divorces his wife, except on the ground of unchastity, causes her to commit adultery; and whoever marries a divorced woman commits adultery."* The condemnation of marital infidelity is so strong that it overrides all other considerations. To reject ones wife was an act with grave social and religious consequences in Judaic society. A man driven by the shame of his own origins and the rumor of his mother's marital infidelity as the cause of that shame might come to have strong feelings about marital fidelity.

Emotional remoteness from the parent held responsible for one's troubles is not an unexpected consequence. Angry persons often manifests their anger with a parent by refusing to use the common terms of endearment, mother or father. The search for emotional distance sometimes takes the form of calling the parent by their first name in an effort to verbally eradicate any emotional connection. The Jesus saga seems to suggest something similar in Jesus' references to his mother as "woman" instead of mother whenever he addressed her. According to the *Oxford Bible*, "the term woman is a form of solemn and respectful address." (53) This seems curious. In Aramaic, the word for mother, *imah*, is quite distinct from the word for woman, *ishah*. As best as can be determined, there is no meaning in Aramaic where the word *ishah* can be used as a respectful or solemn form of address in the same way as, for example, the term "lady" may be used to designate a woman of higher virtue or rank. The Aramaic language clearly uses *ishah* in a manner that the word "boy" might be used despairingly to designate the lower status of a Black male.

The Gospels record that Jesus spoke directly to women on only seven occasions. On four of those occasions, he uses the term "woman" in address; in the other three he either used their first name [Martha] or called them "daughter" or in the case of the women weeping in the street, "daughters of Jerusalem." He used the term "woman" in addressing the hemorrhaging woman, the woman who had five husbands and was living in sin, and the stranger who sat listening to him preach about adultery. Only at the resurrection at the tomb does he use woman to address someone he knows, and that in the case of Mary Magdalene whom he calls by name when she fails to recognize him.

It would seem that Jesus used personal forms of address for women when he wished to do so, but reserved the more remote term "woman" for females he did not know or whom he held in lesser esteem as, for instance, when addressing the adulteress ad the hemorrhaging woman. The linguistic evidence further suggests that the term "woman" was not a formal and respectful form of address, but quite the opposite. It was a term lacking in respect and was condescending in its implication of the lower status of females in Israelite society. This seems evident from *Luke* 22:55-57 recounting of the story of Peter's betrayal of Jesus. A servant-girl approaches Peter and stares at him saying, *"This man was also with him."* Eager to save his own skin from the authorities, Peter turns on the woman and shouts, *"Woman, I do not know him!"* Jesus' use of "woman" to address his mother may represent an attempt to deny or not recognize the maternal connection to the very woman who he held responsible for his public shame as a *mamzer* and the poor treatment at the hands of his fellow Jews who denied him participation in the congregation of Nazareth when he was a young man.

NOTES

1. John Dominic Crossan, *The Historical Jesus: The Life of a Mediterranean Jewish Peasant* (San Francisco: Harper Collins, 1992), 138.

2. David Aune, "Magic in Early Christianity," *Aufstieg und Niedergang der romishcen Welt* vol. 23 (February, 1980), 1517; see also Crossan, 309.

3. Jan Assmann, *Moses the Egyptian* (Cambridge, MA: Harvard University Press, 1997), 61-62.

4. *Exodus* 8:26.

5. A.S. Yahuda, "The Osiris Cult and the Designation of Osiris Idols in the Bible," *Journal of Near Eastern Studies*, vol. 3 (1944), 196.

6. Assmann, 69

7. W.W. Tarn, *Hellenistic Civilization* (New York: Meridian Books, 1961), 235

8. Morton Smith, *Jesus The Magician* (New York: Barnes and Noble, 1993), 69.

9. Ibid.

10. Crossan, 141.

11. Ibid.

12. Ibid., 156.

13. Smith, 9.

14. E.A. Wallis Budge, *Osiris and the Egyptian Resurrection* (New York: Dover Publications, 1973), vol. II, 169.

15. Smith, 79.

16. Budge, 181

17. Ibid., 170.

18. Ibid., 182.

19. Smith, 48.

20. Smith, 48. See also the *Greek Magical Papyrus*, Book 7:222-232 and Book 8: 65 as cited in Smith.

21. Smith, 46.

22. Smith, 47.

23. In one version of the story regarding Jesus' illegitimacy it is alleged that his father was someone named Pantera who may have been a Sidonian archer named Tiberius Julius Abdes Pantera who served in Palestine about the time of Jesus' birth and later saw duty on the Rhine. Jesus is sometimes referred to as "Ben Pantera" in the polemical literature. In the case of the reference to him as "Ben

Stada," it is probably a play on words describing Mary as *"s'tat da,"* i.e.. "the one who has turned away from her husband."

24. Smith, 151.

25. Hyam Maccoby, *The Mythmaker: Paul and the Invention of Christianity* (New York: Barnes and Noble, 1998), 107.

26. Ibid.

27. *The New American Bible*, "New Testament: Letter to the Galatians," (New York: Catholic Book Publishing Company, 1992), 292.

28. For a detailed account of the beliefs and rituals of the Attis cult see the *Encyclopedia Britannica*, 11th Edition (1910), vol. 2, p. 886-887.

29. *Matthew* 26: 26-28.

30. Smith, 122.

31. *John* 6:51

32. *John* 5:54-56

33. Smith, 150.

34. See the F.L. Griffith and Herbert Thompson, *The Demotic Magical Papyrus of London and Leiden* (London: H. Grevel and Co., 1904) for this and other texts.

35. Ibid., p. 15, as quoted in Smith, 122.

36. *John* 6:52.

37. Smith, 123.

38. Maccoby, 110.

39. Crossan, 324.

40. Ibid. 354-355.

41. *The New American Bible*, "Matthew," p. 14.

42. Ibid.

43. Sir Alan Gardiner, "The Baptism of Pharaoh," *Journal of Egyptian Archaeology*, 36 (1950), 3-12.

44. Rosalie David, *The Cult of the Sun: Myth and Magic in Ancient Egypt* (New York: Barnes and Noble, 1998), 100.

45. Ibid.

46. Ibid., 101.

47. Gardiner, "Baptism of Pharaoh," 12.

48. Ibid., 6.

49. Ibid., 7.

50. *Matthew* 3:16-17.

51. *The New American Bible*, "Matthew," 14.

52. David, 102.

53. *The New Oxford Annotated Bible* (New York: Oxford University Press, 1991), 127.

6

Postscript

The conclusion of the inquiry undertaken in this book may not be welcomed by many Christians for whom Jesus is god incarnate and whose teachings represent the gift of a new theology to the world in which the gospel is that man lives on after death. The ancient Coptic Christians, familiar with much of the evidence presented in these pages, concluded long ago that God had prepared the land of Egypt in a special way for his Christ. The Copts may be justified in their conclusion, for Egyptian religion more than Judaism seems the more appropriate wellspring of Christianity. For our part we must admit at the very least that Jesus' teachings and rituals did not represent a unique theological creed, and certainly not an historical singularity as theologians sometimes claim. Jesus' teachings and his ritual practice were indistinguishable in every important detail from those espoused and practiced by the Osiris-Isis faith that had existed for thousands of years before Jesus was born, and which was the dominant pagan cult in Palestine and throughout the Roman world at the time that Jesus lived. Jesus did not invent the theological precepts of what later became Christianity, but seems only to have adopted them from the Osirans. His followers then spread them throughout the world in the name of Jesus Christ.

This raises the question of Jesus' motivation in espousing a pagan creed for Jews to adopt. No historical analysis can ever address the truth of the claim that Jesus was god incarnate. We are left only with an examination of Jesus' behavior and how that might be explained in *human* terms. The adoption of Osiran precepts and rituals represents a strong rejection of the precepts and rituals of the Judaism of Jesus' day. It is this rejection of his religious tradition that intrigues so much. As an explanation I have suggested that Jesus' felt shame at being a *mamzer*, a conclusion that can be reasonably inferred from his pronouncements and behavior toward his mother and family. This shame amplified his feeling of rejection by religious authorities during his early years and turned to anger. It was his anger, not Jesus' concern for the religious reform of Judaism, that caused Jesus to reject the religious authority of Judaism and to espouse a pagan creed for his fellow Jews. Saint Francis Xavier, a reformer of the Catholic Church in the Middle Ages, threatened to "use the hammers forged in the temple to destroy the temple," to use the arguments of the religious establishment against itself to reform the church. Jesus seems to have had much the same thing in mind.

Strongly held beliefs are not easily questioned by those who hold them, nor is it easy for person to abandon beliefs once thought to be true. This examination of the origins of Christianity will undoubtedly bring into question the deeply held beliefs of some people. That was never my intention. Belief is always to be distinguished from knowledge, as history is always to be distinguished from theology. The *intensity* of religious belief is always unrelated to its *content*, to what is actually believed. Religious belief is not just a "leap of faith" rooted in some prior rational analysis that the intellect cannot grasp but that the "leap" can further illuminate. Put simply, religious belief is not another way of knowing. Belief is instead the overt manifestation of a deep human psychological need to make sense of the unknown that reason cannot satisfy. The need to believe dwells deeply within us, and when it confronts reason it is often reason that gives way.

The difficulty is that the psychological need to believe can become so deeply integrated into the human psyche that the very definition and survival of the self becomes one with sustaining the belief as true. It is unrealistic to expect the mind to remain open to new evidence under these circumstances. The debate about what is true or not simply vanishes, replaced by a stronger adherence to the belief. This is precisely what Nietzsche meant when he wrote, "Every tradition grows evermore vulnerable—the more remote is its origin—the more confused that origin is. The reverence to it increases from generation to generation. The tradition finally becomes holy and inspires awe." We need not remain consigned, however, to such forgetfulness. The enemy of discovery is not ignorance but the presumption of knowledge, the certainty that the answer is already known. And so it has been that the reverence, longevity, and institutions of Christianity themselves have become impediments to the acceptance of new thinking about the events surrounding the origins of Christianity. But what is divine need not always be reduced to human terms. The choice to do so or not is always available. This book is an attempt to reexamine the most basic questions surrounding the origins of *Christianity as history*. The hope is that we will see more clearly with reason just what it is we believe through faith.

Selected Bibliography

Ahlstrom, G. and Edelmann, D. "Merneptah's Israel." *Journal of Near Eastern Studies* 44 (1985): 59-62.

Albright, William F. *The Archaeology of Palestine*, 4th ed. London (1960).

Albright, Wiliam F. "Moses Out of Egypt." *Biblical Archaeologist* 36 (February, 1973): 48-76.

Albright, William F. "The Earliest Forms of Hebrew Verse." *Journal of the Palestine Oriental Society* 2 (1922): 69-86.

Albright, William F. "A Revision of Early Hebrew Chronology." *Journal of the Palestine Oriental Society* 1 (1922): 49-79.

Albright, William F. "Historical and Mythical Elements in the Story of Joseph." *Journal of Biblical Literature* 37 (1918): 111-143.

Aldred, Cyril. *Akhenaten: King of Egypt*. London: Thames and Hudson, 1988.

Allen, E. L. "Jesus and Moses in the New Testament." *Expository Times* (Edinburgh) 67 (October 1955-September 1956): 104-106.

Alter, Robert. *The Art of Biblical Narrative*. New York: Basic Books, 1981.

Anati, E. *Palestine Before The Hebrews*. London: 1963.

Angus, S. *Religious Quests of the Greek and Roman World*. Cambridge: Cambridge University Press, 1967.

Arkell, A.J. "The Prehistory of the Nile Valley." *Handbuch der Orientalistik* 8 (1975): 1.2

Armstrong, Karen. *A History of God*. New York: Ballantine Books, 1993.

Assmann, Jan. *Moses The Egyptian*. Cambridge, MA: Harvard University Press, 1997.

Aune, David E. "Magic in Early Christianity." in *Augstieg und Niedergang der romischen Welt* in Hildegard Temporini and Wolgang Hesse (eds.), Berlin and New York: Walter de Gruyter, 1980: 1507-1557.

Austin, M.M. *Greece and Egypt in the Archaic Age*. Cambridge: Cambridge University Press, 1970.

Baines, John. "Interpretation of Religion: Logic, Discourse, Rationality." Gottingen: *Gottinger Miszellen* (1976): 25-54.

Barb, A.A. "The Survival of Magic Arts." in Arnaldo Momigliano (ed.), *The Conflict Between Paganism and Christianity in the Fourth Century*. Oxford: Clarendon Press, 1963: 100-125.

Bauer, Walter. *Orthodoxy and Heresy in Earliest Christianity*. Philadelphia: Fortress Press, 1971.

Bell, H.I. "Roman Egypt from Augustus to Diocletian." *Chronique d'Egypte* 13 (1938):

347-363.

Bell, H.I. "Hellenic Culture in Egypt." *Journal of Egyptian Archaeology* 8 (1922): 139-155.

Benko, Stephen. "Early Christian Magical Practices." in Kent Richard (ed.), *Society of Biblical Literature Seminar Papers*. Chico, CA: Scholars Press, 1982: 9-14.

Blackman, A.M. "Oracles in Ancient Egypt." *Journal of Egyptian Archaeology* 11 (1925): 249-255.

Bokser, Baruch. "Wonder-Working and the Rabbinic Tradition: The Case of Hanina Ben Dosa." *Journal for the Study of Judaism* 16 (1985): 42-92.

Bonnel, R.G. and Tobin, V.A. "Christ and Osiris: A Comparative Study." in S. Groll (ed.), *Pharaonic Egypt*. Jerusalem: 1929.

Brandon, S.G.F. *Creation Legends of the Ancient Near East*. New York: Charles Scribner's Sons, 1969.

Brandon, S.G.F. *Man and His Destiny in the Great Religions*. Toronto: Toronto University Press, 1962.

Brandon, S.G.F. *The Judgement of the Dead*. New York: Charles Scribner's Sons, 1969.

Brandon, S.G.F. "The Ritual Technique of Salvation in the Ancient Near East." in S.G.F. Brandon. *The Savior God*. Manchester, England: Manchester University Press, 1963.

Brandon, S.G.F. *Religion in Ancient History*. New York: Charles Scribner's Sons, 1969.

Breasted, James H. *The Dawn of Conscience*. New York: Charles Scribner, 1947.

Breasted, James. H. *Development of Religion and Thought in Ancient Egypt*. New York: Harper and Brothers, 1959.

Breasted, James H. *Ancient Records of Egypt* (4 vols) Chicago: Univesity of Chicago Oriental Institute, 1906.

Brown, Peter. *The World of Late Antiquity*. New York: W.W. Norton, 1989.

Buber, Martin. *Moses: The Revelation and the Covenant*. Amherst, NY: Humanity Books, 1998. Budge, E.A. Wallis. *From Fetish to God in Ancient Egypt*. New York: Dover Publications, 1988.

Budge, E.A. Wallis. *Egyptian Ideas of the Afterlife*. New York: Dover Publications, 1995.

Budge, E.A. Wallis. *The Egyptian Book of the Dead*. New York: Dover Publications, 1967.

Budge, E.A. Wallis. *Osiris and the Egyptian Resurrection*. (2 vols.) New York: Dover Publications, 1973.

Budge, E.A. Wallis. *Egyptian Magic*. New York: Dover Publications, 1971.

Butcher, E.L. and W.M.F. Petrie. "Early Forms of the Cross from Egyptian Tombs." *Ancient Egypt* 3 (1916): 97-109.

Carrington, P. *The Early Christian Church*. Cambridge: Cambridge University Press, 1957.

Cerny, Jaroslav. "Consanguineous Marriages in Pharaonic Egypt." *Journal of Egyptian Archaeology* 40 (1954): 23-29.

Cerny, Jaroslav. *Ancient Egyptian Religion*. Westport, CT: Greenwood Press, 1979.

Charlesworth, James H. *Jesus Within Judaism: New Light From Exciting Archaeological Discoveries*. New York: Anchor Bible Library, 1988.

Childs, Brevard A. "The Birth of Moses." *Journal of Biblical Literature* 84 (June, 1965): 109-122.

Clayton, Peter A. *Chronicle of the Pharaohs*. London: Thames and Hudson, 1994.

Coats, George W. "What Do We Know Of Moses." *Interpretation: A Journal of Bible and Theology* 27 (January, 1974): 91-94.

Collins, John J. *Between Athens and Jerusalem: Jewish Identity in the Hellenistic Diaspora*. New York: Crossroads Press, 1983.

Crossan, John Dominic. *The Historical Jesus: The Life of a Mediterranean Jewish Peasant*. San Francisco: Harper Collins, 1992.

David, Rosalie. *The Ancient Egyptians: Religious Beliefs and Practices*. London: Routledge and Kegan Paul, 1982.

David, Rosalie. *The Cult of the Sun: Myth and Magic in Ancient Egypt*. New York: Barnes and Noble, 1998.

Douglas, Mary. *In The Wilderness: The Doctrine of Defilement in the Book of Numbers*. Sheffield, England: Sheffield Academic Press, 1993.

Doyle, R.J. and Lee, Nancy C. "Microbes, Religion, and War." *Canadian Journal of Microbiology* 32 (March, 1986): 193-203.

Dyson, Stephen L. "Native Revolts in the Roman Empire." *Historia* 20 (1961): 239-274.

El-Amir, Mustafa. "Monogamy, Polygamy, Endogamy, and Consanguinity in Ancient Egyptian Marriage." *Bulletin of the Egypt Institute in Cairo* 62 (1964): 103-108.

Erman, Adolf. *Life In Ancient Egypt*. New York: Dover Publications, 1971.

Everyday Life Through the Ages. London: Reader's Digest Association Ltd., 1992.

Fairman, H.W. "Tutankhamun and the End of the 18th Dynasty." *Antiquity* 46 (1972): 15-18.

Fairman, H.W. "The Kingship Rituals of Egypt." in S.H. Hooke (ed.), *Myth, Ritual, and Kingship*. Oxford: Oxford University Press, 1958: 74-104.

Falk, Harvey. *Jesus the Pharisee: A New Look at the Jewishness of Jesus*. New York: Paulist Press, 1985.

Fischer, H.G. "An Example of Atenist Iconoclasm." *Journal of the American Research Center in Egypt* 13 (1976): 131-132.

Freud, Sigmund. *Moses and Monotheism*. New York: Vintage Books, 1939.

Freyne, Sean. "The Charismatic." in John J. Collins and George W.E. Nicklesburg (eds.), *Ideal Figures in Ancient Judaism: Profiles and Paradigms*. Chico, CA: Scholars Press, 1980: 223-258.

Gabriel, Richard A. and Metz, Karen S. *From Sumer to Rome: The Military Capabilities of Ancient Armies*. (Westport, CT: Greenwood Press, 1991.

Gabriel, Richard A. and Metz, Karen S. *A History of Military Medicine* (2 vols.) Westport, CT: Greenwood Press, 1992.

Gabriel, Richard A. *The Culture of War*. Westport, CT: Greenwood Press, 1990.

Gabriel, Richard A. *The Great Captains of Antiquity*. Westport, CT: Greewood Press, 2000.

Gardiner, Sir Alan. "The Coronation of King Haremhab." *Journal of Egyptian Archaeology* 39 (1953): 13-16.

Gardiner, Sir Alan. "The Geography of the Exodus: An Answer to Professor Naville and Others." *Journal of Egyptian Archaeology* 10 (1924): 87-96.

Gardiner, Sir Alan. "The Baptism of Pharaoh." *Journal of Egyptian Archaeology* 36 (1950): 3-12.

Gardiner, Sir Alan. *Egypt of the Pharaohs*. London: Oxford University Press, 1961.

Gardiner, Sir Alan. "Notes on the Ethics of the Egyptians." *Ancient Egypt* 2 (1914): 55-58.

Gardiner, Sir Alan. "The Installation of the Vizier." *Recueil de Travaux Relatifs a la Philologie et a l'Aarcheologie Egyptiennes et Assyriennes* 26 (1904): 1-19.

Ghalioungui, Paul. "A Medical Study of Akehanten." *Annales du Service des Antiquities de l'Egypt* 47 (1947): 29-46.

Ghalioungui, Paul. *The House of Life: Magic and Medical Science in Ancient Egypt*. Amsterdam: 1973.

Grant, Michael. *A History of Ancient Israel*. New York: Charles Scribner, 1984.

Grant, Michael. *Jews in the Roman World*. New York: Barnes and Noble, 1995.

Grant, Michael. *An Historians View of the Gospels*. New York: Charles Scribner, 1977.

Green, William Scott. "Palestinian Holy Men: Charismatic Leadership and Rabbinic Tradition." *Aufstieg und Niedergang der romischen Welt* 2.19 (1979): 619-647.

Griffith, F.L. and Herbert Thompson. *The Demotic Magical Paprus of London and Leiden*. London: H. Grevel and Co., 1904.

Griffiths, John Gwyn. "The Egyptian Derivation of the Name Moses." *Journal of Near Eastern Studies* 12 (1953): 225-231.

Griffiths, John Gwyn. *The Origins of Osiris and His Cult*. Leiden: 1980.

Griffiths, John Gwyn. *The Conflict of Horus and Seth From Egyptian Classical Sources: A Study in Ancient Mythology*. Liverpool: 1960.

Grimal, Nicolas. *A History of Ancient Egypt*. London: Basil Blackwell, 1992.

Harrington, Daniel. "The Jewishness of Jesus." *Bible Review* 3.1 (1987): 33-41.

Harrison, R.G. "An Anatomical Examination of the Pharonic Remains Purported to be Akhenaten." *Journal of Egyptian Archaeology* 52 (1966): 95-119.

Hengel, Martin. *The Hellenization of Judea in the First Century After Christ*. Philadelphia: Trinity Press International, 1989.

Hengel, Martin. *Jews, Greeks, and Barbarians*. London: 1980.

Hobson, Christine. *The World of the Pharaohs*. London: Thames and Hudson, 1987.

Hollenbach, Paul W. "The Conversion of Jesus: From Jesus the Baptizer to Jesus the Healer." *Aufstieg und Niedergang der romischen Welt* 2.25 (1982): 196-219.

Hollenbach, Paul W. "Jesus, Demoniacs, and Public Authorities: A Socio-Historical Study." *Journal of the American Academy of Religion* 99 (1981): 567-588.

Horsley, Richard A. "High Priests and the Politics of Roman Palestine: A Contextual Analysis of the Evidence of Josephus." *Journal for the Study of Judaism* 17 (1986): 23-55.

Horsley, Richard A. "Popular Messianic Movements Around the Time of Jesus." *Catholic Biblical Quarterly* 46 (1984): 471-493.

Horsley, Richard A. "Like One of the Prophets of Old: Two Types of Popular Prophets at the Time of Jesus." *Catholic Biblical Quarterly* 47 (1985): 435-463.

Horsley, Richard A. "Popular Prophetic Movements at the Time of Jesus: Their Principle Features and Social Origins." *Journal for the Study of the New Testament* 26 (1986): 3-27.

Horsley, Richard A. "Bandits, Messiahs, and Longshoremen: Popular Unrest in Galilee Around the Time of Jesus." in David J. Lull (ed.), *Society of Biblical Literature Seminar Papers*. Atlanta, GA: Scholars Press, 1988: 183-199.

Hull, John M. "Hellenistic Magic and the Synoptic Tradition." *Studies in Biblical Theology*. Naperville, IL: Allenson Press, 1974.

Jones, Karen Randolph. "The Bronze Serpent in the Israelite Cult." *Journal of Biblical Literature* 87 (September, 1968): 245-256.

Josephus, Flavius. *The Jewish War*. translated by G.A. Williamson. New York: Dorset Press, 1985.

Josephus, Flavius. *The Life and Works of Flavius Josephus*. translated by William Whiston. Philadelphia: John C. Winston Company, 1985.

Kantor, Helene J. "The Early Relations of Egypt With Asia." *Journal of Near Eastern Studies* 1 (1942): 174-213.

Kantor, Helen J. "Further Evidence for Early Mesopotamian Relations With Egypt." *Journal of Near Eastern Studies* 11 (January-October, 1952): 239-246.

Kee, Howard Clark. *Medicine, Miracle and Magic in New Testament Times*. New York: Cambridge University Press, 1986.

Kee, Howard Clark. *Miracle in the Early Christian World: A Study in Sociohistorical Method*. New Haven, CT: Yale University Press, 1983.

Keller, Werner. *The Bible as History*. New York: William Morrow, 1981.

Kirsch, Jonathan. *Moses: A Life*. New York: Ballantine Books, 1998.

Klein, Joel. *In The Name of God*. Westport, CT: Greenwood Press, 2001.

Kilenkow, Anita B. "The Problem of Power: How Miracle Doers Counter Charges of Magic in the Hellenistic World." in George MacRae (ed.), *Society of Biblical Literature Seminar Papers*. Missoula, MT. Scholars Press, 1976: 105-110.

Kraeling, E.G. "The Origins of the Name Hebrew." *American Journal of Semitic Languages and Literature* 58 (1941): 237-253.

Leaney, A.R.C. *The Jewish and Christian World 200 BC to AD 200*. Cambridge: Cambridge University Press, 1983.

Luckenbill, David. D. *Ancient Records of Assyria and Babylonia*. Chicago: Oriental Institute, 1926.

Maccoby, Hyam. *The Mythmaker: Paul and the Invention of Christianity*. New York: Barnes and Noble, 1998.

MacMullen, Ramsay. *Enemies of the Roman Order: Treason, Unrest, and Alienation in the Empire*. Cambridge, MA: Harvard University Press, 1966.

Mankelkern, Solomon. *Veteris Testamenti Concordantiae Hebraicae Atque Chaldaicae*. Jerusalem: Schocken Books, 1967.

Mauss, Marcel. *A General Theory of Magic*. New York: W.W. Norton, 1975.

Meier, John P. *A Marginal Jew: Rethinking the Historical Jesus*. New York: Doubleday Books, 1991.

Metzer, Edward S. "The Parentage of Tutankhamun and Smenkhare." *Journal of Egyptian Archaeology* 64 (1978): 134-135.

Morenz, Siegfried. *Egyptian Religion*. Ithaca, NY: Cornell University Press, 1973.

Morgenstern, Julian. "The Ark, the Ephod and the Tent of Meeting." *Hebrew Union College Annual* 27-28 (1942-1943): 39-49.

Murnane, William J. "On the Accession Date of Akhenaten." *Studies in Honor of George R. Hughes*. Chicago: Oriental Institute, 1977: 163-167.

Murnane, William J. "The El-Amarna Boundary Stele Project." University of Chicago, *Oriental Institute Annual Report* (1983-1984): 13-16.

Murnane, William J. "The Hypothetical Coregency Between Amenhotep III and Akhenaten: Two Observations." *Serapis* 2 (1970): 17-21.

Naville, Edouard. "The Geography of the Exodus." *Journal of Egyptian Archaeology* 10 (1924): 18-39.

New American Bible. New York: Catholic Book Publishing House, 1992.

Overmann, Andrew J. "Who Were the First Urban Christians? Urbanization in Galilee in the First Century." in David G. Lull (ed.), *Society of Biblical Literature Monograph Series.* Atlanta, GA: Scholars Press, 1988: 160-168.

Peet, T. Eric. *Egypt and the Old Testament.* Liverpool: University Of Liverpool, 1922.

Peters, F.E. *The Harvest of Hellenism.* New York: Barnes and Noble, 1996.

Petrie, W.M.F. "The Royal Magician." *Ancient Egypt* 3 (1925): 65-70.

Plastaras, James. *The God of Exodus: The Theology of the Exodus Narratives.* Milwaukee: Bruce Publishing Co., 1966.

Pritchard, James B. *Ancient Near Eastern Texts Relating to the Old Testament.* Princeton: Princeton University Press, 1955.

Raven, Maarten J. "Wax in Egyptian Magic and Symbolism." *Oudheidkundige Mededelingen uit het Rijksmuseum van Oudheden te Leiden* 64 (1983): 7-47.

Redford, Donald. *Akhenaten: The Heretic King.* Princeton: Princeton University Press, 1984.

Redford, Donald. "The Monotheism of the Heretic Pharaoh." *Biblical Archaeological Review* (May-June, 1987): 16-32.

Rees, B.R. "Popular Religion in Graeco-Roman Egypt: The Transition to Christianity." *Journal of Egyptian Archaeology* 36 (1950): 86-100.

Reeves, C.N. "Akhenaten After All?" Gottingen: *Gottinger Miszellen* 54 (1982): 61-72.

Robins, Gay. "A Critical Examination of the Theory that the Right to the Throne of Ancient Eygpt Passed Through the Female Line in the 18th Dynasty." Gottingen: *Gottinger Miszellen* 62 (1983): 67-78.

Robins, Gay and Shute, C.C.D. "Wisdom From Ancient Greece." *Discussions in Egyptology.* Oxford: (1985) 35-42.

Rostovtzeff, M. "The Foundations of Social and Economic Life in Hellenistic Times." *Journal of Egyptian Archaeology* 6 (1920): 161-178.

Rowley, H.E. "Early Levite History and the Question of the Exodus." *Journal of Near Eastern Studies* 3 (1944): 73-78.

Rowley, H.E. *From Joseph To Joshua.* London: Oxford University Press. 1948.

Saldarini, Anthony J. "Political and Social Roles of the Pharisees and Scribes in Galilee." in David J. Lull (ed.), *Society of Biblical Literature Seminar Papers.* Atlanta,GA: Scholars Press, 1988: 200-209.

Samson, Julia Ellen. "Akhenaten's Coregent and Successor." Gottingen: *Gottinger Miszellen* 57 (1982): 57-60.

Samson, Julia Ellen. Akhenaten's Coregent Anheperure-Nefernefruaten" Gottingen: *Gottinger Miszellen* 53 (1981): 51-54.

Samson, Julia Ellen. "The History of the Mystery of Akhenaten's Successor." *L'Egyptologie* 2 (1979): 291-298.

Samson, Julia Ellen. "Akhenaten's Successor." Gottingen: *Gottinger Miszellen* 32 1979): 53-58.

Sandman, Maj. "Texts From the Time of Akhenaten." *Bibliotheca Aegyptiaca Brussels* 8 (1938): 43-51.

Schulman, A.R. "Some Remarks on the Military Background of the Amarna Period." *Journal of the American Research Center in Egypt* 3 (1964): 57-70.

Scott, Joseph and Lenore Scott. *Egyptian Hieroglyphics for Everyone: An Introduction to the Writing of Ancient Egypt.* New York: Barnes and Noble, 1993.

Smallwood, E.M. *The Jews Under Roman Rule.* Leiden: 1976.

Smend, Rudolf. *Yahweh, War and Tribal Confederation: Reflections Upon Israel's Earliest History.* translated by May Gray Rogers. Nashville and New York: Abingdon Press, 1970.

Smith, Jonathan. "The Temple and Magician." in J.Z. Smith. *Map Is Not Territory.* Leiden: Brill, 1978: 172-189.

Smith, Morton. "The Jewish Elements in Magical Papyri." in Kent Richards (ed.), *Society of Biblical Literature Seminar Papers*. Atlanta, GA: Scholars Press, 1986: 455-462.

Smith, Morton. *Jesus The Magician*. New York: Barnes and Noble, 1993.

Speigelberg, W. "The Shepherd's Crook and the So-Called Flail or Scourge of Osiris." *Journal of Egyptian Archaeology* 15 (1939): 80-83.

Spong, John Shelby. *Liberating the Gospels: Reading the Bible With Jewish Eyes*. San Francisco: Harper, 1996.

Tarn, W.W. *Hellenistic Civilization*. New York: Meridian Books, 1961.

Tcherikover, V. *Hellenistic Civilization* and the Jews. Philadelphia: 1975.

Te Velde, H. "Some Remarks on the Structure of Egyptian Divine Triads." *Journal of Egyptian Archeology* 57 (1971): 80-86.

Theodorides, Aristide. "The Concept of Law in Ancient Egypt." in J.R. Harris (ed.), *The Legacy of Egypt*, 2nd ed. Oxford: Oxford University Press, 1971: 291-322.

Towers, J.R. "Was Akhenaten a Monotheist Before His Accession?" *Ancient Egypt* 4 (1931): 97-100.

Velikovsky, Immanuel. *Worlds In Collision*. New York: Dell Publishing Co., 1965.

Velikovsky, Immanuel. *Oedipus and Akhenaten*. New York: Doubleday and Company, 1960.

Vermes, G. "Baptism and Jewish Exegesis: New Light From Ancient Sources." *New Testament Studies* 4 (1958): 309-319.

Ward, Colleen A. and Beaubrun, Michael H. "The Psychodynamics of Demon Possession." *Journal for the Scientific Study of Religion* 19 (1980): 201-207.

Weigall, Arthur. *The Life and Times of Akhenaten* (1923).

Weisfeld, Israel H. *This Man Moses*. New York: Bloch Publishing Company, 1966.

Wiener, H.M. "The Historical Character of the Exodus." *Ancient Egypt* 4 (1926): 104-115.

Wilson, S. *Saints and Their Cults: Studies in Religious Sociology, Folklore, and History.* Cambridge: Cambridge University Press, 1983.

Wolfe, Alan. "The Opening of the Evangelical Mind." *Atlantic Monthly* (October, 2000): 55-75.

Wright, G.E. (ed.) *The Bible and the Ancient Near East.* New York: 1961.

Yahuda, A.S. "The Osiris Cult and the Designation of Osiris Idols in the Bible." *Journal of Near Eastern Studies* 3 (1944): 194-197.

Yeiven, S. "Canaanite Ritual Vessels in Egyptian Cultural Practices." *Journal of Egyptian Archaeology* 62 (1976): 110-114.

Yerushalmi, Yosef Hayim. *Freud's Moses: Judaism Terminable and Interminable.* New Haven and London: Yale University Press, 1991.

Young, Allan. "The Anthropologies of Illness and Sickness." *Annual Review of Anthropology* 11 (1982): 257-285.

Zivotofsky, Ari Z. "The Leadership Qualities of Moses." *Judaism* 43 (Summer, 1994): 258-269.

978-0-595-35087-2
0-595-35087-9

Printed in the United Kingdom
by Lightning Source UK Ltd.
111737UKS00001B/150